Microsoft

Internet
Explorer 4

Field
Guide

Stephen L. Nelson   **Microsoft** Press

The Microsoft Internet Explorer 4 Field Guide *is divided into four sections. These sections are designed to help you find the information you need quickly.*

Environment

Terms and ideas you'll want to know to get the most out of Microsoft Internet Explorer. All the basic parts of the Internet are shown and explained. The emphasis here is on quick answers, but most topics are cross-referenced so that you can find out more if you want to.

Diagrams of key Internet components, with quick definitions, cross-referenced to more complete information.

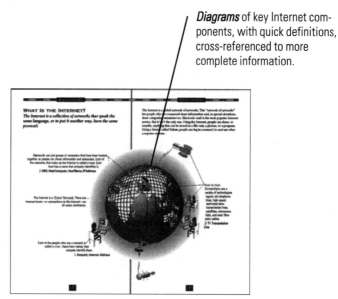

Tips

Watch for these as you use this Field Guide. They'll point out helpful hints and let you know what to watch for.

13.88

Microsoft
Internet
Explorer 4

Field
Guide

PUBLISHED BY
Microsoft Press
A Division of Microsoft Corporation
One Microsoft Way
Redmond, Washington 98052-6399

Library of Congress Cataloging-in-Publication Data
Nelson, Stephen L., 1959-
   Microsoft Internet Explorer 4 Field Guide / Stephen L
Nelson.
      p.   cm.
   Includes index.
   ISBN 1-57231-741-8
   1. Microsoft Internet Explorer.   2. Internet (Computer network)
I. Title.
TK5105.883.M53N45   1998
004.67'8--dc21   97-42102
                                       CIP

Printed and bound in the United States of America.

1 2 3 4 5 6 7 8 9 MLML 3 2 1 0 9 8

Distributed to the book trade in Canada by Macmillan of Canada,
a division of Canada Publishing Corporation.

A CIP catalogue record for this book is available from the British Library.

Microsoft Press books are available through booksellers and distributors
worldwide. For further information about international editions, contact your
local Microsoft Corporation office. Or contact Microsoft Press International
directly at fax (425) 936-7329. Visit our Web site at mspress.microsoft.com.

Acquisitions Editor: Susanne Freet
Project Editor: Anne Taussig

15 Internet Explorer A to Z

An alphabetic list of commands, tasks, terms, and procedures.

Cross-references to related topics.

Step-by-step guides to performing most Internet tasks.

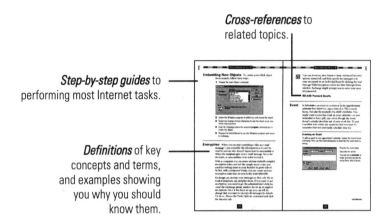

Definitions of key concepts and terms, and examples showing you why you should know them.

143 Troubleshooting

A guide to common problems—how to avoid them and what to do when they occur.

155 Quick Reference

Useful indexes, including a full list of menu commands, shortcut keys, and more.

171 Index

A complete reference to all elements of the Field Guide.

Introduction

In the real world, you need
practical solutions. Fast.
This Field Guide provides
just these sorts of lightning-
quick answers. But take two
minutes now and read the
introduction. It explains
how this unusual little
book works.

What Is a Field Guide?

Sometime during grade school, my parents gave me a field guide to
North American birds. With its visual approach, its maps, and its numerous
illustrations, that guide delivered hours of enjoyment. The book also helped
me better understand and more fully appreciate the birds in my neighborhood. And the small book fit neatly in a child's rucksack. But I'm getting
off the track.

This book works in the same way as that field guide. It organizes information
visually with numerous illustrations. And it does this in a way that helps
you more easily understand and enjoy working with the Internet using a
personal computer and Microsoft Internet Explorer 4.0. For new users, the
Field Guide provides the essential information necessary to start using the
Internet. But the Field Guide isn't only for beginners. For experienced users,
the Field Guide provides concise, easy-to-find descriptions of Internet Explorer tasks, terms, and techniques.

When You Have a Question

Let me explain then how to find the information you need. You'll usually
want to flip first to the Environment section, which is really a visual index.
You find the picture that shows what you want to do or the task you have a
question about. If you want to know how to connect to the Internet, you flip
to pages 4 and 5, which talk about different ways you connect your personal
computer to the Internet.

Next you read the captions that describe the parts of the picture. Say, for
example, that you want to use an Internet service provider. On page 4, there's
a caption that describes what Internet service providers are.

You'll notice that some captions use boldface terms or are followed by
additional **boldface** terms. These refer to entries in the second section,
Internet Explorer A to Z, and provide more information related to the
caption's contents.

Internet Explorer A to Z is a dictionary of more than 200 entries that define terms and describe tasks. (After you've worked with the Internet a bit or if you're already an experienced user, you'll often be able to turn directly to this section.) So if you have just read the caption that talks about Internet service providers, you'll see the term **Connection Wizard** in boldface, indicating a cross-reference. If you don't know what the Connection Wizard is, you can flip to the Connection Wizard entry in Internet Explorer A to Z.

When an entry in Internet Explorer A to Z appears as a term within another entry, I'll **boldface** it the first time it appears in that entry. For example, as part of describing what the Connection Wizard is, I might tell you that after you run the Connection Wizard, you should be able to browse the **World Wide Web.** In this case, the words World Wide Web appear in bold letters—alerting you to the presence of another entry explaining the term World Wide Web. If you don't understand the term or want to do a bit of brushing up, you can flip to the entry for more information.

When You Have a Problem

The third section, Troubleshooting, describes problems that new and casual users of Internet Explorer often encounter. Following each problem description, I list one or more solutions you can employ to fix the problem.

When You Wonder About a Command

The Quick Reference at the end of the Field Guide describes the **Internet Explorer, Outlook Express,** and **Telnet** menu commands, as well as the **FTP** commands. (You enter the FTP commands using a command prompt.) If you want to know what a specific command does, turn to the Quick Reference. Don't forget about the Index either. You can look there to find all references in this book to any single topic.

Conventions Used Here

I have developed a few conventions to make using this book easier for you. Rather than use wordy phrases such as "Activate the File menu and then choose the Print command" to describe how you choose a menu command, I'm just going to say, "Choose the File menu's Print command."

Another thing. I've rather freely tossed out **uniform resource locators,** or URLs. And to make them stand out on the page, I've *italicized* them. OK, now I know that you might not know what these URL things are yet. But after you've noodled around a bit—and learned how to use them—you'll be happy I provided them. They give you the precise directions for finding cool stuff on the Internet.

When I give commands you type at a command prompt—such as in **UNIX** or using the **FTP** client—I also *italicize* the command name.

Finally, I want to let you know about a couple of conventions I used when creating the figures for this book, so that you won't get confused if the figures you see here look a little different than the figures you see on your screen. First of all, you might notice that all of the web pages you see in this book include the Internet Explorer application window, instead of taking up the whole screen. This is because I find the menu bar and the Microsoft Windows Taskbar handy when I'm working in Internet Explorer, so I like to keep them displayed. If you agree with me, you can click the Fullscreen button to switch out of full screen mode. The other thing I want to say about the figures in this book is that they might look a little different than what you have on your screen depending on which version of Internet Explorer you installed. This book applies to all of the versions, but when I was writing this book, I used the full installation, which is why you might see some buttons or features here that you didn't install.

Environment

Need to get oriented
quickly? Then the
Environment is the place to
start. It defines the key
terms you'll need to know
and the core ideas you
should understand as you
begin exploring the
Internet—and using Internet
Explorer 4.0.

What Is the Internet?

The Internet is a collection of networks that speak the same language, or to put it another way, use the same protocol.

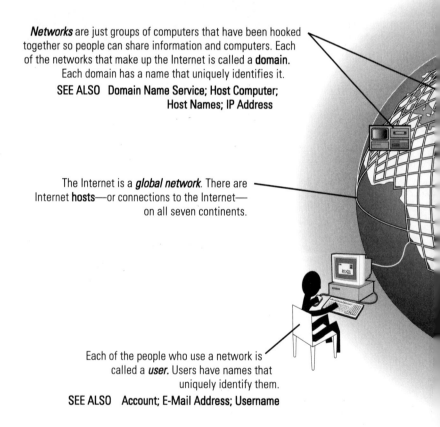

Networks are just groups of computers that have been hooked together so people can share information and computers. Each of the networks that make up the Internet is called a **domain**. Each domain has a name that uniquely identifies it.

SEE ALSO   Domain Name Service; Host Computer; Host Names; IP Address

The Internet is a **global network**. There are Internet **hosts**—or connections to the Internet— on all seven continents.

Each of the people who use a network is called a **user**. Users have names that uniquely identify them.

SEE ALSO   Account; E-Mail Address; Username

The Internet is a global network of networks. This "network of networks" lets people who are connected share information and, in special situations, share computing **resources** too. Electronic mail is the most popular Internet service. But it isn't the only one. Using the Internet, people can share, or transfer, anything that can be stored in a **file**: text, a picture, or a program. Using a feature called **Telnet,** people can **log on** (connect) to and use other computer systems.

Host-to-Host Connections use a variety of technologies: regular old telephone lines, high-speed, dedicated data-transmission lines, satellites, microwave links, and even fiber-optic cables.

SEE ALSO   T1 Transmission Line;
T3 Transmission Line

Connecting to the Internet

To use any resource or service on the Internet, you first need to connect to it.

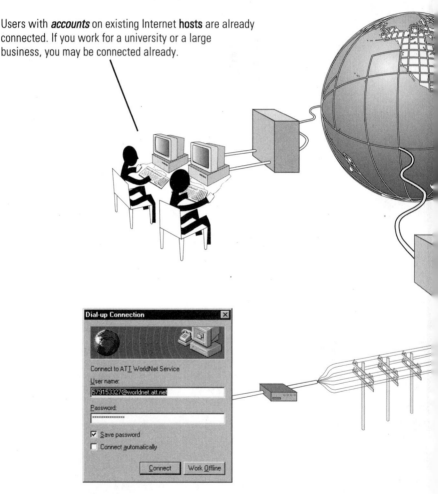

Users with *accounts* on existing Internet **hosts** are already connected. If you work for a university or a large business, you may be connected already.

Internet service providers offer pay-for-use accounts on computers that are connected directly to the Internet. With a modem and a personal computer, you can often connect to a local service provider.

SEE ALSO   Connection Wizard; Dial-Up Networking; Shell Account

People get connected in a variety of ways. The cheapest and easiest way to get connected is to use your personal computer and **modem** to connect by way of an **Internet service provider.** The most expensive, most complicated, and most powerful way to get connected, or "wired," is to have your network become one of the Internet's permanent networks.

SEE ALSO   Connection Wizard

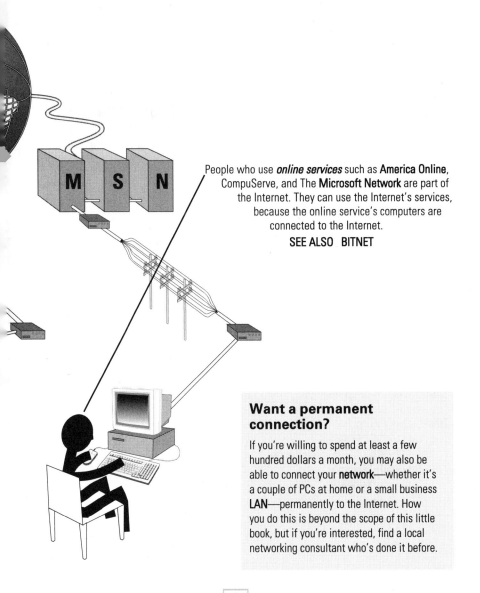

People who use *online services* such as **America Online**, CompuServe, and The **Microsoft Network** are part of the Internet. They can use the Internet's services, because the online service's computers are connected to the Internet.

SEE ALSO   BITNET

Want a permanent connection?

If you're willing to spend at least a few hundred dollars a month, you may also be able to connect your **network**—whether it's a couple of PCs at home or a small business **LAN**—permanently to the Internet. How you do this is beyond the scope of this little book, but if you're interested, find a local networking consultant who's done it before.

Sending Electronic Mail

The Internet's most popular service is electronic mail, or e-mail.

E-mail programs such as **Outlook Express** let you create and send mail messages. They also let you read and organize mail messages others send you.

Addresses give the names of both the **user** and host.
SEE ALSO   Domain Names;
E-Mail Address

Interest lists are electronic **mailing lists** of people who have a special interest in a specific topic. By joining an interest list—putting your name on the mailing list— you can see tons of messages related to a topic.
SEE ALSO   FAQ; Lurk;
Netiquette

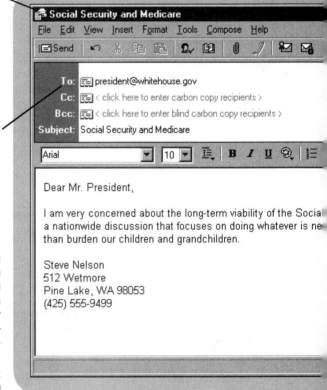

Social Security and Medicare

File   Edit   View   Insert   Format   Tools   Compose   Help

Send

To: president@whitehouse.gov
Cc: < click here to enter carbon copy recipients >
Bcc: < click here to enter blind carbon copy recipients >
Subject: Social Security and Medicare

Arial   10   B I U

Dear Mr. President,

I am very concerned about the long-term viability of the Socia
a nationwide discussion that focuses on doing whatever is ne
than burden our children and grandchildren.

Steve Nelson
512 Wetmore
Pine Lake, WA 98053
(425) 555-9499

To send someone electronic mail, you create a mail message. The message includes the name and **e-mail address** of the person to whom the message should be delivered, the text of the message, and your name and e-mail address. Once you send your message, it is passed from **host** to host until the message reaches its destination.

Mail **gateways** connect the Internet to other networks such as **America Online,** CompuServe, GEnie, and MCI Mail, so you can send mail messages to users of these **outernet** services, too.

SEE ALSO   E-Mail; Outlook Express

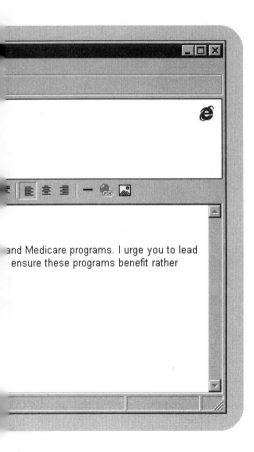

and Medicare programs. I urge you to lead
ensure these programs benefit rather

How secure are e-mail messages?

It's not easy to intercept e-mail messages, and most people wouldn't intercept others' mail intentionally, but you should know it is possible to eavesdrop on e-mail messages. For this reason, some people encrypt messages.

Newsgroups

Newsgroups resemble interest lists. In newsgroups, mail messages are collected and organized by topic. The difference is that newsgroup mail messages, called **articles,** aren't distributed but are stored on central computers, called news **servers.** You decide which newsgroup articles you want to read—they aren't sent to you.

World Wide Web

The World Wide Web is a collection of multimedia documents that are connected by hyperlinks.

Uniform resource locators are addresses that identify the locations of World Wide Web pages.

Hyperlinks connect different World Wide Web documents. Hyperlinks are usually identified by underlining or color. To move to another document, you just click the hyperlink. Hyperlinks can connect World Wide Web documents on different **hosts**.

Graphics images commonly appear in World Wide Web documents. Some images are also hyperlinks to image files. You can view and **download** these files by clicking.

SEE ALSO GIF; JPEG; Viewer

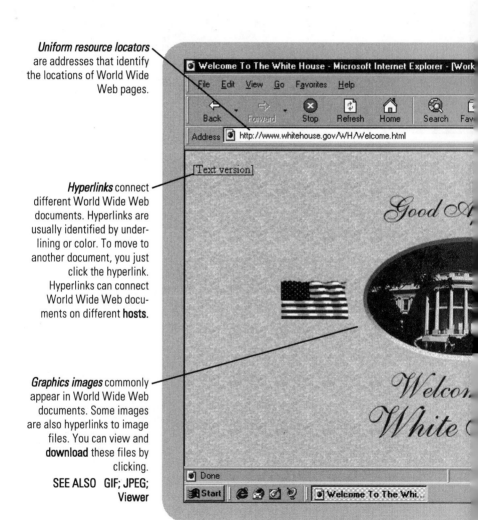

To view **World Wide Web** documents, you need a web browser, such as **Microsoft Internet Explorer,** and a **Dial-Up Networking** connection or an account on an **online service** that provides World Wide Web browsing. Browsing web pages traditionally required you to manually click **hyperlinks** and enter **uniform resource locators.** You can still navigate the Web in this way, but Internet Explorer 4.0 also lets you automatically retrieve and receive web sites using **subscriptions** and **channels.**

The Fullscreen button lets you change the look of your screen by making more or less room for viewing web pages.

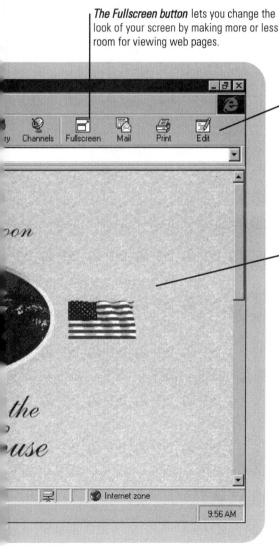

Toolbars in Internet Explorer provide buttons you can click to navigate the World Wide Web and make use of other Internet features. Which toolbar buttons you have depends on how you installed Internet Explorer.

SEE ALSO Installing Internet Explorer

World Wide Web documents can include text, pictures, and just about anything else that can be stored in a computer file.

FileTransfers

File transfers represent another way to share information on the Internet.

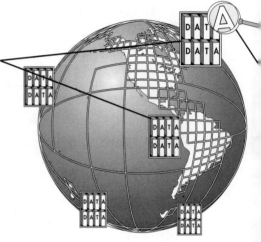

Data archives exist all over the world. Using the Internet, you should be able to access publicly accessible data archives.

SEE ALSO   Anonymous FTP; Netiquette

Compression utilities shrink files so they take less time to transmit over the Internet. When you receive a file that has been compressed, you need to decompress ("unshrink") it.

SEE ALSO   Bandwidth; Bits; PKZIP; ZIP

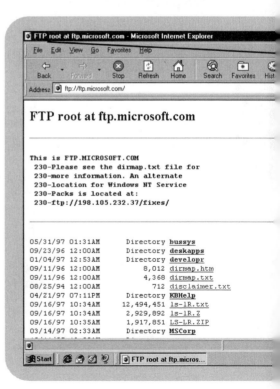

FTP root at ftp.microsoft.com - Microsoft Internet Explorer

File   Edit   View   Go   Favorites   Help

Back   Forward   Stop   Refresh   Home   Search   Favorites   Hist

Address   ftp://ftp.microsoft.com/

FTP root at ftp.microsoft.com

```
This is FTP.MICROSOFT.COM
230-Please see the dirmap.txt file for
230-more information. An alternate
230-location for Windows NT Service
230-Packs is located at:
230-ftp://198.105.232.37/fixes/
```

```
05/31/97 01:31AM        Directory bussys
09/23/96 12:00AM        Directory deskapps
01/04/97 12:53AM        Directory developr
09/11/96 12:00AM            8,012 dirmap.htm
09/11/96 12:00AM            4,368 dirmap.txt
08/25/94 12:00AM              712 disclaimer.txt
04/21/97 07:11PM        Directory KBHelp
09/16/97 10:34AM       12,494,451 ls-lR.txt
09/16/97 10:34AM        2,929,892 ls-lR.Z
09/16/97 10:35AM        1,917,851 LS-LR.ZIP
03/14/97 02:33AM        Directory MSCorp
```

Start   FTP root at ftp.micros...

File transfers let you copy files between Internet hosts. To transfer files between Internet hosts, you use the file transfer protocol, or **FTP.** You can copy almost anything that can be stored in a file: programs (for a variety of computers and operating systems), images, and, of course, plain text files.

SEE ALSO   FTP; Internet Explorer

File location tools such as **Gopher, Archie,** and **search engines** make it easier to find files you want—even if it means you need to search **hosts** all over the world.

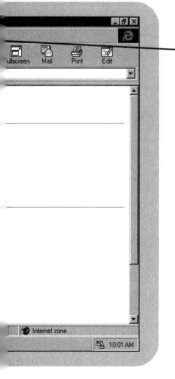

File retrieval usually requires you to start a **client,** such as **FTP,** or a web **browser,** such as **Internet Explorer,** and then to issue a command indicating that you want to get a file. To retrieve a file using the FTP client, you have to give the precise name of the file. To retrieve a file using Internet Explorer, you just click the file's name in a list.

SEE ALSO   Downloading Files

11

Telnetting

Internet Explorer also allows you to remotely connect, or log on, to other Internet hosts.

You use *Telnet* to connect to another Internet **host.** Once you connect to the other host, you log on by providing a **username** and a **password.**

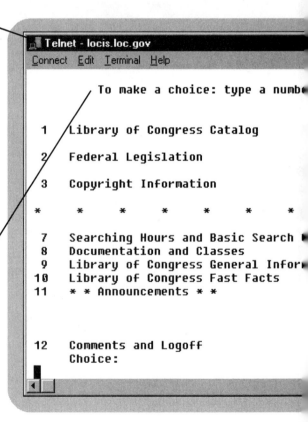

```
Telnet - locis.loc.gov
Connect   Edit   Terminal   Help

              To make a choice: type a numb

    1    Library of Congress Catalog

    2    Federal Legislation

    3    Copyright Information

    *    *    *    *    *    *    *

    7    Searching Hours and Basic Search
    8    Documentation and Classes
    9    Library of Congress General Infor
    10   Library of Congress Fast Facts
    11   * * Announcements * *


    12   Comments and Logoff
         Choice:
```

Menu systems usually appear once you successfully log on to the other Internet host. Menu systems guide you through the services you can use.

Once you've logged on, you can use the other computer system—or at least the parts of it you're allowed to use. One important factor to keep in mind is that computers and networks operate in different environments. So things may look a bit different once you connect. For example, if you're used to working in Microsoft Windows and you **telnet** to a **UNIX** network, the screens and the commands will look different. If you've telnetted to a different country, you may even see a different language.

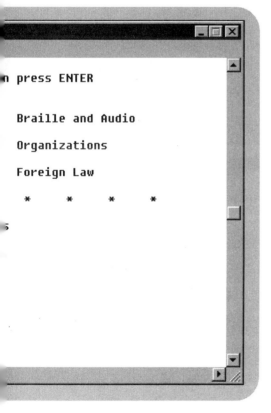

Making a telnet connection typically requires you to click a **hyperlink** that points to a telnet site or to supply the **uniform resource locator** for a telnet site.

Three Telnet tips

When you telnet to another host, you should pay particular attention to three things: how you should disconnect once you're done, how to get help within the system, and the name and **e-mail address** of the person you should contact if a problem arises.

Internet Explorer

A to Z

Maybe it's not a jungle out
there. But you'll still want to
keep a field guide close at
hand. Internet Explorer
A to Z, which starts on the
next page, lists in
alphabetic order the tools,
terms, and techniques
you'll need to know.

Access Provider SEE Internet Service Provider

Account

To use an **Internet service provider,** you typically sign up for an account. This account, in effect, is how you identify yourself to the Internet service provider's **host computer.** As part of setting up your account, the system administrator gives you a **username** that you use to identify yourself to the system and a **password** so that you can get into the system.

Active Channel

An active channel is a channel web site that you've specified as one you want to regularly view. By making the channel active, the channel web site will regularly deliver content to your desktop. You can view a channel in the Microsoft Internet Explorer browser window, as a full screen, on an **Active Desktop,** or as a **screen saver.**

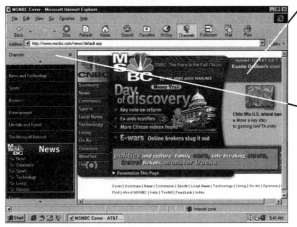

This is how an active channel's web pages look in the Internet Explorer window.

The Channel bar provides clickable buttons you can use to work with channels.

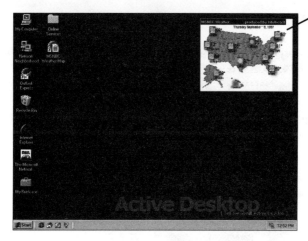

This weather map image, which sits on the Microsoft Windows desktop, is also an active channel.

SEE ALSO   Subscriptions; Web browsing

Active Desktop

An Active Desktop is a Windows **desktop** that you've essentially turned into one, big **web page.** This sounds a bit confusing, however, so let me explain. The screen that you see after you start (and possibly log on to) Windows is the Windows desktop. This desktop, as you probably know, shows the Start button, the Taskbar, and clickable shortcut icons you can use to start programs or view Windows folders.

An Active Desktop is a sort-of supercharged desktop to which you've added a web page background or some portion of a web page—perhaps from a **channel.** With an Active Desktop, you can display web pages, or at least pieces of them, right on your desktop. You can also use a web page as your desktop background (also known as wallpaper).

Adding Items to Your Desktop with an Add To Active Desktop Button

To add a web page to your Active Desktop, display the web page that you want to add. Then click the web page's Add To Active Desktop button. (You may need to hunt about a bit for this button.) Internet Explorer adds the web page to your Active Desktop as an Active **Desktop item.**

continues

Active Desktop *(continued)*

Adding Items to Your Desktop Without the Add To Active Desktop Button

To add an item to your Active Desktop for a web page that doesn't show an Add To Active Desktop button, follow these steps:

1 Right-click the Active Desktop.

2 Choose the Properties command. Windows displays the Display Properties dialog box.

3 Click the Web tab.

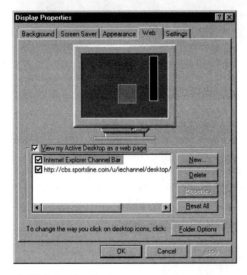

4 Click the New button.

5 When Windows prompts you, enter the **uniform resource locator** of the web page you want to use as a desktop item on your Active Desktop. Click OK when you are asked to confirm the addition of the new desktop item.

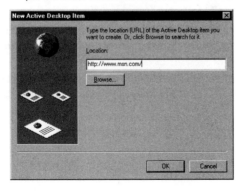

Updating Desktop Items

To update the desktop items shown on your Active Desktop, right-click the desktop to display the Active Desktop shortcut menu. Choose the Active Desktop command to display the Active Desktop submenu. Then choose the Update Now command.

About the Active Desktop submenu's other commands

The Active Desktop submenu also provides two other commands. The View As Web Page command, which works like a toggle switch, lets you alternately view your Active Desktop as a Windows desktop or as a web page in a browser window. (Experiment with this command to see how it works.) The Customize My Desktop command displays the Display Properties dialog box.

Removing Desktop Items

To remove a desktop item from your Active Desktop, follow these steps:

1 Right-click the Active Desktop.

2 Choose the Properties command. Windows displays the Display Properties dialog box.

3 Click the Web tab.

4 Click the desktop item you want to remove.

5 Click Delete.

Using an HTML Document for Desktop Wallpaper

To use an HTML document you've stored locally on your computer as wallpaper, or background, follow these steps:

1 Right-click the Active Desktop.

2 Choose the Properties command. Windows displays the Display Properties dialog box.

3 Click the Background tab.

continues

Active Desktop *(continued)*

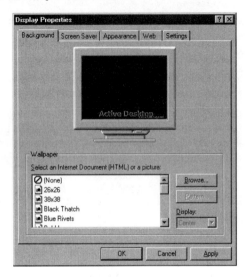

4 Click the Browse button. Windows displays the Browse dialog box.

5 Use the Browse dialog box's buttons and boxes to locate the HTML document.

6 Double-click the HTML document. Windows adds the HTML document to the list box that shows available wallpaper selections for your Active Desktop.

7 Select the HTML document from the Wallpaper list box.

8 Click OK.

Removing or Replacing HTML Wallpaper

You can easily remove or replace an HTML document you've used for wallpaper. To remove wallpaper from the desktop background, click the Background tab in the Display Properties dialog box (as described in the preceding instructions), select the None entry from the Wallpaper list box, and click OK. (The None entry appears at the top of the list.)

To replace the existing HTML wallpaper with some other wallpaper, click the Background tab in the Display Properties dialog box and then select another wallpaper from the Wallpaper list box. After you've made your selection, click OK.

ActiveX

ActiveX is the name Microsoft has given to a technology that lets people share information and programs. Using ActiveX, for example, you can view a Microsoft Word word-processor document with Internet Explorer. You can move information you create from one program (such as Microsoft Excel) to another program (such as Microsoft PowerPoint). And you can run miniature ActiveX programs inside a web browser such as Internet Explorer. Well, I should say, you can if the browser supports ActiveX technology. (If you remember the Microsoft term OLE, you may find it helpful to know that ActiveX replaces OLE. If you don't remember or know the term OLE, don't worry.)

Address Book

You use the Address Book to store the names and e-mail addresses of the people to whom you want to send **e-mail.** You can also store people's addresses, telephone numbers, and other information.

Opening the Address Book

To open the Address Book, you typically first start Microsoft Outlook Express and then click the Address Book button. You can also open the Address Book from within Outlook Express by choosing the Tools menu's Address Book command. From within Internet Explorer, you open the Address Book by choosing the Go menu's Address Book command.

continues

Address Book *(continued)*

Storing an E-Mail Address

You can store an e-mail address in your Address Book in several ways. If you want to add the name of the person who has already sent you a message, display the message and right-click the sender's name. When Outlook Express displays the shortcut menu, choose the Add To Address Book command.

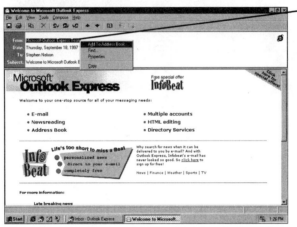

Right-click the sender's name in the message window to display a shortcut menu with a command for adding the sender's name to your Address Book.

If you haven't already received a message (or can't find a message) from the person you want to add to your Address Book, open the Address Book and then follow these steps:

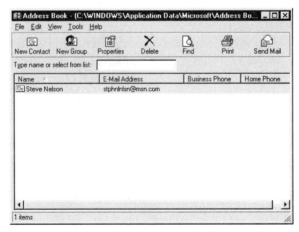

1 Click the New Contact button. Outlook Express displays the Properties dialog box.

2 Click the Personal tab if it isn't already displayed.

3 Use the Name boxes—First, Middle, Last, Display, and Nickname—to enter the person's name. (The name you enter in the Display box shows up in your e-mail messages to that person.)

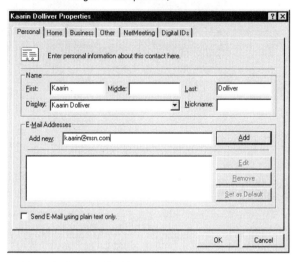

4 Enter the full e-mail address for the person in the Add New box, and then click the Add button.

5 Optionally, if this person uses an e-mail client that works with plain text only, select the Send E-Mail Using Plain Text Only check box.

6 Optionally, click the Home, Business, Other, NetMeeting (also called Conferencing), or Digital ID tabs and use their buttons and boxes to describe the person in more detail.

7 When you finish describing the person, click OK.

Printing E-Mail Information

You can print the e-mail name and address information that you collect. To do this, select the name of the person whose information you want to print. Then click the Print button.

Using an E-Mail Address in a Message

You can use e-mail address information from the Address Book in several ways. The simplest method is to enter the person's Display name in the To box in the New Message window. (This is the name you entered in the Display box in step 3 in the preceding instructions.) When you do this, Outlook Express retrieves the e-mail address from the Address Book and then uses the e-mail address to send the message.

continues

Address Book *(continued)*

If you type enough of someone's Display name for Outlook Express to recognize, it will complete the name for you.

If you're not sure of the Display name you used, open the Address Book, select the name of the person to whom you want to send an e-mail message, and then click the Send Mail button. Outlook Express opens a message form window and fills in the To box with the name of the person you selected. To complete your message, type the message subject, write the message, and click the Send button.

Updating or Deleting an E-Mail Address

To update e-mail address information you've stored in the Address Book, open the Address Book, select the e-mail address you want to change, and then click the Properties button. If you want to delete an e-mail address, click the e-mail address and then click the Delete button.

Importing E-Mail Addresses You've Stored in Another Client's Address Book

If prior to using Outlook Express you used another e-mail client, you may already have an address book of e-mail names and addresses. Fortunately, you may be able to extract this information from the other client's address book. To do this, follow these steps:

1 Start Outlook Express.

2 Choose the File menu's Import command, and then choose the Import submenu's Address Book command. Outlook Express displays the Address Book Import Tool dialog box.

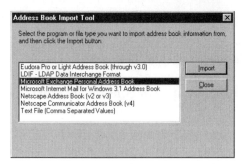

3 Select the list box entry that corresponds to the type of e-mail client and address book you previously used.

4 Click Import. Then follow the on-screen instructions. (The instructions vary depending on what you want to import.)

AltaVista

AltaVista is an Internet **search engine,** or search service. It works like a giant index of the Internet. To use AltaVista, you specify a word or phrase you want to look up. (You do this using a search form, which is just a web page that provides boxes and buttons.) AltaVista then looks up the word or phrase in its index and displays a list of **hyperlinks** that point to web pages that use the term. To move to a page, you click its hyperlink. (For step-by-step instructions about how to use AltaVista and other search engines, refer to the search engine A to Z entry.)

Like other search engines, AltaVista makes it possible for you to find information on the World Wide Web. For this reason, you'll definitely want to learn how to use AltaVista or one of the other search engines.

SEE ALSO   Yahoo!

America Online

America Online is one of many online services that gives you access to a lot of different resources, including the Internet. However, I'm not going to describe how you access the Internet specifically with America Online (or any other **Internet service provider**) in this book.

I will say that if you want to **e-mail** someone who subscribes to America Online, you just need to tag the America Online **domain name,** aol.com, onto the end of his or her **username.** For example, if you want to send an e-mail message to someone's America Online address and his e-mail name is johndoe, you put the e-mail name together with America Online's domain name to create the **e-mail address:**

johndoe@aol.com

SEE ALSO   **Netiquette; Outernet**

Anchor

The **hyperlinks** in **World Wide Web** documents—the same ones you click to move from web page to web page—are sometimes called anchors. I don't really know why. But then I don't make the rules.

Anonymous FTP

Anonymous FTP just means that someone without an **account** on an Internet **host** can still **FTP.** In other words, if an Internet host allows anonymous FTPs, you can connect to the host (no matter who you are) and start FTPing.

Using Internet Explorer for Anonymous FTP

To use anonymous FTP, simply enter the **uniform resource locator** of the FTP site in the Address box of Internet Explorer. When you do, Internet Explorer displays the FTP site's folders, or directories.

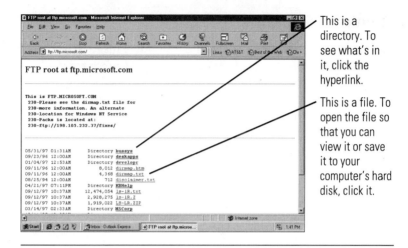

This is a directory. To see what's in it, click the hyperlink.

This is a file. To open the file so that you can view it or save it to your computer's hard disk, click it.

List of Useful Anonymous FTP Sites

There are a bunch of anonymous FTP sites. I can't list them all, but here's a starter list of uniform resource locators that you can use to track down and explore some of the more popular and useful FTP sites for Windows users:

Uniform resource locator	What the site offers
ftp://ftp.microsoft.com	Selected Microsoft Corporation programs including several for Windows
ftp://ftp.ncsa.uiuc.edu	National Center for Supercomputing Applications stuff from the University of Illinois at Urbana-Champaign—such as the NCSA Mosaic web **browser**
ftp://rtfm.mit.edu	**FAQs** maintained by the Massachusetts Institute of Technology on just about everything

Apple Macintosh

The world of microcomputers is essentially divided into two camps, the Apple Macintosh camp and the PC camp. PC stands for "personal computer," and although Macintoshes are also personal computers, the term *PC* always refers to IBM computers and IBM compatibles.

This book focuses on connecting PCs that are running Windows 95 (and later versions) to the Internet. You won't find anything here specifically about Apple Macintosh computers, or "Macs" as they are called by their loyal users. But much of what I say here also applies to Mac users.

Archie

Archie is a tool people use for finding **files** at **FTP** sites. In essence, what you do is tell Archie that you're interested in files with a specific name or files that have a specified string in their names (a string is just a chunk of text). Archie goes out and looks through a list of files at an Archie **server.** Then it builds a list of files (and their locations) that match your description and sends you the list. If you see something you want to retrieve, you use **anonymous FTP** to retrieve the file.

Using Archie with E-Mail

Windows users have several ways to use Archie. One method is to send an **e-mail** message to one of the Archie servers. To do this, you need to find out the **domain name** of an Archie server. For example, maybe you discover there's an Archie server named *archie.rutgers.edu.* (There actually is an Archie server with this domain name.) Once you have this information, send an e-mail message to Archie at the Archie server. For example, to send an e-mail to archie.rutgers.edu, you send the e-mail to *archie@archie.rutgers.edu.* Oh, one other thing. Your e-mail message needs to use the message text

```
find filename
```

The **filename** should be either the filename or a portion of the filename. For example, if you want to find files that use the word "mouse," your message text is

```
find mouse
```

A little while later—it could easily be an hour—you'll get back an e-mail message that lists uniform resource locators (URLs) for files that use the word or string you specified. You then use FTP to retrieve the file you want.

Using Archie with Telnet

If you installed the Windows **telnet** client on your computer, the simplest method for finding files with an Archie server is to telnet to the Archie server (netiquette says you should almost always use one that's close to your host), sign on using Archie as the **username** but without a **password,** and then use its commands. After you've telnetted to the Archie server and you see the Archie command prompt, for example, enter the *find* command:

```
find filename
```

Finding an Archie Server

You need to know an Archie server's domain name before you can send it e-mail or try to telnet to it, of course. So here's a list of Archie servers that were active as I was writing this book:

Server	Location
archie.au	Australia
archie.univie.ac.at	Austria
archie.belnet.be	Belgium
archie.bunyip.com	Canada
archie.cs.mcgill.ca	Canada
archie.funet.fi	Finland
archie.cru.fr	France
archie.th-darmstadt.de	Germany
archie.ac.il	Israel
archie.unipi.it	Italy
archie.wide.ad.jp	Japan
archie.hana.nm.kr	Korea
archie.kornet.nm.kr	Korea
archie.sogang.ac.kr	Korea
archie.uninett.no	Norway
archie.icm.edu.pl	Poland
archie.rediris.es	Spain
archie.luth.se	Sweden
archie.switch.ch	Switzerland
archie.ncu.edu.tw	Taiwan
archie.doc.ic.ac.uk	United Kingdom
archie.hensa.ac.uk	United Kingdom
archie.sura.net	USA (Maryland)
archie.unl.edu	USA (Nebraska)
archie.internic.net	USA (New Jersey)
archie.rutgers.edu	USA (New Jersey)
archie.ans.net	USA (New York)

Getting an up-to-date list of Archie servers

You can get a list of active Archie servers like the one shown above by sending the one-word message "servers" to an Archie server.

continues

Archie *(continued)*

Using Archie with Internet Explorer

Not surprisingly, several web servers also maintain Archie server catalogs. These web servers provide web page forms that let you search their catalogs. To use this method for locating a file with Archie, use a **search service** such as AltaVista to build a current list of Archie catalog web sites. (To do this, search on the term "Archie.") Then click the appropriate hyperlink to get the closest Archie web server and follow its on-screen instructions.

SEE ALSO   Gopher

ARPA

ARPA is an acronym for Advanced Research Projects Agency. ARPA is the central research and development agency for the U.S. Department of Defense. You're wondering, of course, what any of this has to do with the Internet. Well, quite a lot actually. Over the past 20 years, ARPA funded many computer-related projects that shaped the computer industry and the Internet. BSD (Berkeley Software Distribution) **UNIX**, is one example, and the **TCP/IP** protocol is another. Most significant, however, is the fact that ARPA funded the ARPANET **network** that served as the starting point of the Internet.

SEE ALSO   Gulf War

Article

People often call the messages that get posted to a **newsgroup** "articles." This name makes sense if you think of a newsgroup as an electronic newspaper or magazine. If newspapers and magazines contain articles, so too must newsgroups.

If people respond to an article by posting another article, the first article and its responses are called a **thread.**

Authentication

Authentication refers to the process by which an Internet service provider's **host computer** makes sure that you and your computer are who you say you are. You can't just **log on** to an **Internet service provider's** host computer. You have to provide your name or a **username.** And you need to provide a **password.**

By the way, making the **PPP** (Point-to-Point Protocol) connection is a little easier if you're making a PPP connection to a host computer that supports one of the authentication **protocols,** PAP (Password Authentication Protocol) or CHAP (Challenge Handshake Authentication Protocol). (Don't get bummed out by kooky protocol acronyms. I find them just as irritating as you do.) You can store your username and your password with the other Internet connection information. When Windows logs on to the Internet service provider's computer, it supplies your username and password. So you don't have to. If this is your situation, you don't need to tell Windows to bring up a terminal window after you make the PPP connection.

Backbone

The term *backbone* refers to the extremely fast, high-bandwidth connections over which a majority of Internet traffic moves. In the United States of America, SprintNet (a commercial firm) maintains the backbone, although not all that long ago, NSFnet (a government agency) maintained the backbone. Other countries typically have their own backbones.

Bandwidth

When people talk about the Internet, they use the term *bandwidth* to describe how much data can be transmitted in a given time, say a second. In these cases, people usually calibrate the bandwidth in **bits per second** (bps), kilobits per second (Kbps), or megabits per second (Mbps).

People who like big words use the term bandwidth to describe people who can absorb or transmit lots of information really quickly. (Ideally, then, you want to be a high-bandwidth person.)

SEE ALSO   Bit; T1 Transmission Line; T3 Transmission Line

Baud

Baud (rhymes with "Maude") is the measure of data-transmission speed. When it comes to **modem** speeds, people often talk about the "baud rate," although modem speed is not measured in bauds. Actually, modem speed is measured by the number of data bits that can be transmitted in a second. That is, modem speed is measured in **bits per second** (bps), kilobits per second (Kbps), or megabits per second (Mbps).

SEE ALSO   Cable Modem; Modem

BBS

BBS is an acronym for bulletin board system. In essence, BBSs work like those cork bulletin boards you see at the local grocery store. You know the ones I mean, right? The same ones where ancient Winnebagos are offered for sale, where 12-year-old kids offer baby-sitting services, and rewards are offered for lost dogs.

The only difference between cork bulletin boards and BBSs is that you post and read BBS messages electronically by using your computer and a **modem**. All you need is a communications program like Windows's **HyperTerminal** application to connect to a BBS. If you want to make a connection, the best approach is to call the BBS operator and ask how you're supposed to make it.

By the way, BBSs aren't necessarily part of the Internet—although they can be. You do often see them being advertised slyly on the Internet, however. For example, some BBSs post graphics files and utilities in **newsgroups**. The BBS operators hope that once you see these newsgroups, you'll learn about their graphics files and utilities and you'll be willing to pay to **download** them.

Bit

Bit stands for "binary digit." A bit is the smallest unit of computer data. Each bit represents a 1 or a 0. Bits are grouped in bunches of eight to form bytes, and bytes represent real information, such as letters and the digits 0 through 9. Modem transmission speeds, by the way, are measured in **bits per second.**

SEE ALSO   Baud; Kilobit; Kilobyte

Bitmap

A bitmap is simply a pattern of colored dots. On your screen, each colored dot is created as a pixel of light and is described by one or more **bits** (binary digits). This sounds like a bunch of gobbledy-gook, but if the colored dots are arranged in the right way, you get a picture such as the one shown below.

The reason I mention this is that you can **download** bitmap files in various file formats from newsgroups and **FTP** sites. Both **GIF** and **JPEG** formats are common, for example.

As a young man, I almost got the chance to shake President Kennedy's hand. But this other kid—I think his name was Bill— cut in front of me. And I lost my chance.

As a point of historical reference, I'll also mention that probably the best known bitmaps were those created in the late nineteenth century by the French impressionist Georges Seurat. In this case, however, the colored dots were created by brushstrokes on canvas rather than by pixels of light. And you thought this book was just about computers...

BITNET

BITNET is an acronym—almost. It stands for "Because It's Time NETwork." BITNET started in the early 1980s and was mostly a university-oriented **network**. It networks mainly IBM and DEC mainframes and minicomputers. Usually used for mail and **file** transfers, BITNET's **LISTSERV**-based **mailing lists** are numerous and still very active. But today BITNET is diminishing in light of the Internet's popularity.

You don't really need to know anything about BITNET. But you sometimes hear the term being tossed around.

Bits Per Second

Your computer and all the other computers connected to the Internet use **bits** (binary digits) to store information. If you could look at your hard disk with a disk viewing utility (and they do exist), you would see a bunch of 1s and 0s. As a practical matter, you don't really need to know anything about bits (or bytes either). But they are sort of relevant because **modem** speeds are described in bits per second, or bps. A 2400bps modem can theoretically spew or swallow a stream of slightly more than a couple thousand 1s and 0s every second. A 14,400bps, or 14.4Kbps, modem can theoretically spew or swallow a stream of roughly fourteen thousand 1s and 0s every second. The faster the modem, the easier and faster it is to move data around the Internet. If you want to browse the **World Wide Web,** for example, you need a modem that goes at least 28.8Kbps.

SEE ALSO   Baud

Bookmarks

Bookmarks are just **uniform resource locators** (URLs) that you've told your web browser you want it to memorize. Some people call these memorized URLs bookmarks because that's what **Netscape Navigator** calls them. And some people call these memorized URLs **favorites** because that's what **Internet Explorer** calls them.

BPS SEE Bits Per Second

Bridge

You don't need to know the term *bridge* to use the Internet. But the term may come in handy at a cocktail party or a coffee klatsch. A bridge is a device that connects two **networks** so they appear to be a single, larger network.

SEE ALSO   Gateway

Browser

A browser is a program that lets you look at **World Wide Web**
documents. **Netscape Navigator** is a browser, for example. And so
is **Internet Explorer,** which is what this book is mostly about. You
now know everything you need to know to use the term *browser*
with confidence. But since you're still reading, let me tell you a bit
more. Most browsers let you browse, or view, both the graphics and
text components of World Wide Web documents. But there are
also browsers that let you look at just the text. For example, if you
have a **shell account** and your **Internet service provider** supports
the Lynx program, you can view just the text components of World
Wide Web documents. (You might want to do this, for example, if
your connection to the Internet is slow—say less than 28.8Kbps—
or if you are really only interested in the text portions of the documents you are viewing.) What's more, more browsers (including
Internet Explorer) let you do more than just look at web pages.
You can also view the contents of **anonymous FTP** sites, work with
Gopher, view **GIF** and **JPEG** graphics images, and open text files.

Byte SEE Kilobyte

Cable Modems

Cable modems may just be the next big step in data transmission.
A cable modem uses the existing cable company's cables—the same
cables that bring premium channels, pay-per-view, home shopping
channels, and dozens of other channels to your home television set.
The sweet part of a cable modem is its speed. A cable modem can
move data from the Internet to your PC at speeds of up to 27 megabits per second, and it can move data from your PC to the Internet
at speeds of up to 1.5 megabits per second. To use a cable modem,
your cable company needs to provide the service. If you're interested, call them and ask.

CERT

CERT, another acronym, stands for Computer Emergency Response Team. Formed by the Advanced Research Projects Agency (**ARPA**) of the U.S. Department of Defense in 1988, CERT worries about the security of Internet **hosts**. So what does CERT do? CERT's main functions are to collect information about security breaches, coordinate responses to security breaches, and train the Internet community about security. It periodically issues advisories on security problems. You don't really need to know anything about CERT—just as you don't need to know anything about the U.S. Army's Delta Force Commandos. But it's reassuring to know that the CERT (and the Delta Force Commandos) exist.

If you're really interested in what CERT does...

For recent advisories, check the newsgroup *comp.security.announce*. Archives of old advisories, as well as security-related programs and information, can be found at *ftp://ftp.cert.org*.

Channel

A channel is a web site that's been designed to deliver its information—its web page content—to your computer automatically. Channels then differ from regular web pages. As you probably know, with a regular web page, you and your web browser connect to a web server and then request a web page. (You typically make this request either by clicking a **hyperlink** or by entering a **uniform resource locator** [URL] in the Address box of your web browser.) A channel, however, works differently. You tell the channel web site that you want to get its information automatically on a regular basis. And then the channel web site does just that.

Adding an Active Channel

To add an active channel to your desktop, start Internet Explorer and click the Channels button to display the Channel bar. Click the Microsoft Channel Guide button to display the Microsoft Active Channel Guide (The Channel Guide is an up-to-date list of hundreds of channel web sites organized by topic.) Select a topic from the list, and then select the channel you want to add to your desktop. When Internet Explorer displays the Channel web page in the browser window, click its Add Active Channel button. Internet Explorer then asks you if and when you want the channel updated. (You make your choice by clicking a button.) And then you're finished.

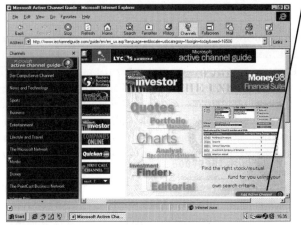

Click this button to add an active channel to your desktop.

Viewing an Active Channel

To view an active channel once you've added it, click the Channels button to display the Channel bar. Then select the channel you've made active.

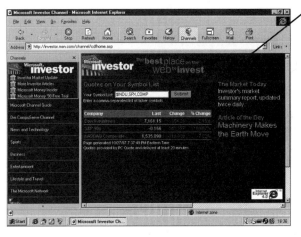

This is how an active channel's information looks. Basically, it's just a regular web page.

Chat

Chat, or more precisely Microsoft Chat, is an Internet **client** add-on that comes with Internet Explorer 4.0. Microsoft Chat lets you send and receive text messages with other users in real time. This means that you can read and respond to what other people type as they're typing. The participants in the chat need only be logged on at the same time and in the same place, called a chat room. To start Microsoft Chat, click the Start button and choose Programs. Then choose the Internet Explorer command to open the Internet Explorer submenu. Choose Microsoft Chat to display the Chat application window. In the dialog box that Chat displays, enter the name of the chat room you wish to participate in and the name of the server holding the chat. If you do not know any chat servers, your Internet service provider should be able to provide you with a list.

If you installed the standard version of Internet Explorer, you didn't install Chat. You need to install it from your CD or download it from the Web.

Circuit-Switching Network

The Internet is not a circuit-switching network. Let me explain. In a circuit-switching network, each network connection requires a dedicated line—a wire, a fiber-optic cable, even a satellite link or a microwave "link." The key feature of a circuit-switching network is that when one computer is talking to another computer, whatever the computers are using to talk to each other is used only for their connection. The most common circuit-switching network is the telephone system. When your computer (the one inside your head) is talking with another computer (perhaps the one inside your boss's head), the telephone line you're using is dedicated to your conversation and nothing else.

Now you might think that this has nothing to do with the Internet. And you're half right. But the reason I brought this up is that knowing what a circuit-switching network is helps you better understand what a **packet-switching network** is, which is what the Internet uses.

Client

When you're talking about the Internet, a client is a software program running on your personal computer that lets you use the Internet. Windows itself comes with several Internet clients, including **FTP, ping,** and **telnet.** And, interesting, Internet Explorer 4.0 doesn't just supply the **Internet Explorer** web browser client but also several other clients, including Microsoft Outlook Express (an e-mail client) and Microsoft Chat (an online chat, or IRC, client). Client software programs work with server software programs that run on the computers you connect to.

SEE ALSO · **Server**

Connections

You can connect to the Internet in several different ways. You can connect by way of a shell account from your work or school. With a shell account, you use a communications application such as **HyperTerminal** to connect to a server and you navigate the Internet textually using UNIX commands.

This Field Guide, however, assumes that you're connecting using Windows's **Dial-Up Networking** feature and **Internet Explorer.** With a Dial-Up Networking account from an Internet service provider you can browse graphical **World Wide Web** documents.

By the way, if you have scads of money, the time, and the technical expertise (or your employer does), you can connect your computer or **network** to the Internet permanently by using a **T1 transmission line.**

SEE ALSO   **FTP; Ping; PPP; SLIP; Telnet**

Connection Wizard

Internet Explorer comes with a Connection Wizard that you can use to set up a new **Dial-Up Networking** connection even after you initially set up Internet Explorer. To use the Connection Wizard, click the Start button and then choose Programs, Internet Explorer, and Connection Wizard. By following the on-screen instructions, the wizard does everything necessary to connect your computer to the Internet. Once you run the wizard, you should be able to browse the **World Wide Web, FTP,** use **Gopher, telnet,** send and receive **e-mail,** and view **newsgroups.**

Cookies

Cookies are files stored on your computer. Remote web **servers** you connect to create cookies to identify you and your web-browsing preferences. This all sounds a bit scary if you think about it very much, but cookies, used correctly, make your web browsing easier. If you frequently connect to a web site that requires a **username** and **password** (say because it charges you money for viewing its content), this information can be stored in a cookie, which means you don't have to log on to the web site every time you visit it.

If you want to be warned before accepting cookies, choose the View menu's Internet Options command and click the Advanced tab. Scroll down the list and click the Prompt Before Accepting Cookies button and then click OK.

Cyberspace

Cyberspace is one of those loosely defined terms that—and this is very handy—most people use to mean whatever they want. If you put me on the spot and made me define it, however, I would say that cyberspace refers to the sum total of the activities and information on the world's computers, particularly the computers that are connected to the Internet or the **outernet.**

DARPA SEE ARPA

Desktop

The desktop is the background screen that appears beneath application windows. In other words, the desktop is what you see after you start and log on to Windows. Internet Explorer 4.0 lets you create an **Active Desktop,** which is a desktop to which you can add **desktop items,** which are basically web pages or portions of **web pages.**

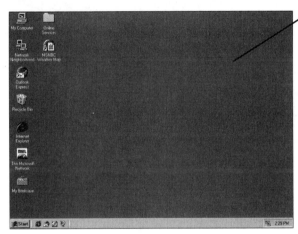

This background is the desktop.

Desktop Items

Internet Explorer 4.0 lets you add portions of **web pages** to your desktop if you've installed and turned on Internet Explorer's **Active Desktop** feature. These portions of web pages are called desktop items.

SEE ALSO   Channel

Dial-Up Networking

To connect to the Internet using the **PPP** or **SLIP** protocol, you need to already have a PPP or SLIP **account** set up with an **Internet service provider.** You also need to use the Windows Dial-Up Networking feature. You use Dial-Up Networking to describe the connection (you do this only one time) and to make the PPP or SLIP connection (you do this every time you connect to the Internet).

continues

Dial-Up Networking *(continued)*

Setting Up a PPP or SLIP Connection

Setting up a PPP or SLIP account is probably one of the most tedious and complicated tasks you'll ever do in Windows, at least as far as the Internet goes. You need to add the **TCP/IP** protocol, configure a **domain name** server, bind the Dial-Up Network adapter to the TCP/IP protocol, and then set up a Dial-Up Networking connection.

Fortunately, you usually shouldn't have to deal directly with the complexity of Dial-Up Networking. If you choose to use one of the Internet service providers that Internet Explorer knows about when you are installing Internet Explorer (and it probably knows about all of the large Internet service providers in your area), the setup program sets up the PPP or SLIP connection automatically. Alternatively, if you already have a Dial-Up Networking connection set up—say you've already been using the Internet—you'll have the choice of using this PPP or SLIP connection.

If you have to do the actual work of describing exactly how the PPP connection or SLIP connection works, ask your Internet service provider for help and specific, step-by-step instructions.

Making a PPP or SLIP Connection

You shouldn't have to do anything special to make a PPP or SLIP connection. If you start Internet Explorer, it checks to see whether a Dial-Up Networking connection is working. If a connection isn't working, Internet Explorer makes the PPP or SLIP connection, prompting for whatever information it needs. (If you need a **password** to connect to your Internet service provider, you'll see a dialog box that asks for this bit of information.)

SEE ALSO   Authentication; Connection Wizard

Digital IDs

A digital ID is a tool you can use to sign your e-mail messages so that the people who receive your messages can be sure they actually came from you. A digital ID also allows you to encrypt your messages so that if a message is intercepted, the thief can't read the scrambled contents. To use a digital ID, you must sign up for one with a commercial firm that supplies and supports digital IDs. You can get more information about how this works by starting Outlook Express, choosing the Tools menu's Options command, clicking the Security tab, and then clicking the Get Digital ID button.

Document Cache

Web browsers such as **Internet Explorer** use something called a document cache, and it's important to understand what the document cache is and how it works. (Internet Explorer calls the document cache by another name, the Temporary Internet Files folder.) The document cache stores copies of **World Wide Web** documents and images on your hard disk so that you don't always have to grab them from some distant World Wide Web **server** in order to view them. Therefore, the document cache also provides a history of the web pages and images you've visited and viewed.

Flushing Your Document Cache

To remove the documents and images stored in your document cache, follow these steps:

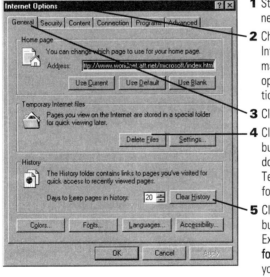

1 Start Internet Explorer, if necessary.

2 Choose the View menu's Internet Options command. Internet Explorer opens the Internet Options dialog box.

3 Click the General tab.

4 Click the Delete Files button to flush your document cache, the Temporary Internet Files folder.

5 Click the Clear History button to erase Internet Explorer's list of the **uniform resource locators** you've visited.

continues

Document Cache *(continued)*

Adjusting Your Document Cache

By default, Internet Explorer uses up to 10 percent of your hard disk for caching. (Internet Explorer may use a smaller percentage if your disk drive is very large.) You can change the size of the document cache by adjusting the percentage of your disk space used to store cached documents and images. To do this, follow these steps:

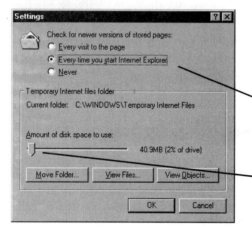

1 Start Internet Explorer.

2 Choose the View menu's Internet Options command.

3 Click the Settings button.

4 Use these buttons to specify when Internet Explorer should retrieve new copies of documents and images.

5 Move the Amount Of Disk Space To Use slider to adjust the size of the document cache.

If you don't want to use cached documents

If you don't want to use cached documents, click the Refresh button or choose the View menu's Refresh command. This tells Internet Explorer to grab a new copy of the document from its World Wide Web server rather than use the cached copy of the document on your hard disk.

Domain Names

The domain name identifies the organization that owns and operates an Internet network. The domain name has the format *organization.type*. The organization part is usually the name or acronym of the organization. For example, *microsoft.com* or *mit.edu*. And organizations have to register their domain with **InterNIC** or another equivalent domain registration service. The type part of the domain name can be one of the following:

Type	What it means
.com	A company or commercial organization. For example, Microsoft's domain name is *microsoft.com.*
.edu	An educational institution. For example, the Massachusetts Institute of Technology's domain name is *mit.edu.*
.gov	A government site. For example, NASA's domain name is *nasa.gov.*
.mil	A military site. For example, the United States Air Force's domain name is *af.mil.*
.net	A gateway or other administrative host for a network. For example, UUNET's domain name is *uu.net.*
.org	An organization that doesn't fit in the other classes of domain types. For example, the Electronic Frontier Foundation's domain name is *eff.org.*

Country types

The domain names of organizations located outside of the United States often use a two-letter country code either in place of or in addition to the three-letter organization-type codes just listed. For example, the two-letter country code for Australia is *au.* And the two-letter country code for Greece is *gr.* (For more examples of country names, see the list of Archie servers provided in the Archie A to Z entry.)

Domain Name Service

Domain Name Service, or DNS, is like a smart, electronic post office. Imagine if all you had to do whenever you wanted to send someone a letter was write the person's name on the outside of the envelope. Then down at the post office, some friendly postal worker looked up the address of the person and mailed the letter. Sounds nice, right? Well, that is basically what DNS does. Because of DNS, you can refer to a host by using its **host name.** DNS then does the work of looking up the host's **IP address** for you.

For example, if you wanted to fiddle-faddle around with the host named *ftp.microsoft.com*, the TCP/IP application you're using would use DNS to look up the correct IP address, which just happens to be 198.105.232.1. (Your machine or a machine you have access to must be configured to use a name **server** that performs the actual looking up.)

Downloading Files

How you move a **file** from the Internet to your PC depends on the way you've connected to the Internet. If you've connected with a **shell account** and you want to move a file from your **Internet service provider's** computer to your PC, you use a communications application like **HyperTerminal**. If you've connected with a **PPP** or **SLIP** connection, you can move the file by using Internet Explorer. In general, to do this, all you need to do is double-click a **hyperlink** that points to the file. Note, too, that if you've already downloaded the file to view it with your browser, you don't need to download the file a second time. To save a permanent copy of the file, simply choose the File menu's Save As command. If you're using an **online service** such as **America Online** or **Microsoft Network,** you use whatever commands the online service's client software provides.

SEE ALSO   Uploading Files

E-Mail

E-mail, or electronic mail, is the Internet's most popular feature. If you have an e-mail client program and access to an e-mail service, you can send electronic mail to just about anyone whose e-mail address you know: the president of the United States (e-mail address: *president@whitehouse.gov*), me (e-mail address: *stphnlnlsn@msn.com*), and even Mick Jagger. (I don't know Mr. Jagger's e-mail address.)

Because e-mail is such a popular Internet feature, Internet Explorer comes with an Internet mail client, **Outlook Express.** If your Internet service provider includes e-mail service, you can use Outlook Express to send and receive e-mail. For this reason, in the paragraphs that follow I'll describe how e-mail works with Outlook Express.

Configuring Outlook Express for E-Mail

If you use the **Connection Wizard** to set up a **Dial-Up Networking** connection with your **Internet service provider**—and this is how you should do this—you don't have to do anything special to configure Outlook Express or your computer for e-mail. The little work that needs to be done (principally identifying the mail **server** and setting up an Inbox folder for your messages) is carried out automatically.

Therefore, if you have trouble getting Outlook Express to pass messages back and forth from your Internet service provider, contact your Internet service provider for assistance.

Creating an E-Mail Message

To create and send an e-mail message to someone, follow these steps:

1 Start Outlook Express.

2 Click the Compose Message button. Outlook Express displays the New Message window

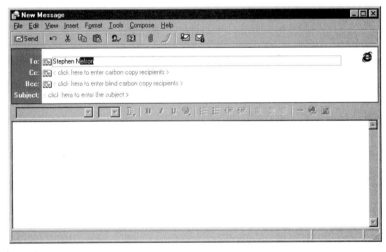

3 Enter the recipient's e-mail address in the To box. If you want to send the message to more than one person, separate the e-mail addresses with semicolons.

4 Optionally, enter the e-mail address of whomever you want to receive a copy of the e-mail message in the Cc box.

5 Optionally, enter the e-mail address of whomever you want to secretly receive a copy of the e-mail message in the Bcc box.

6 Enter a brief description of your message in the Subject box.

7 Use the main message text area to write your message.

8 To send your message when you're finished writing it, click the Send button. If you're already connected to the Internet, clicking Send sends the message to your Internet service provider's mail server (which then begins the process of delivering the message to the recipient). If you're not connected to the Internet—say, because you're working offline—clicking Send places the message in your Outbox.

continues

E-Mail *(continued)*

Formatting e-mail messages

You can format your e-mail messages using the formatting buttons that appear just above the message area. However, the people who receive your messages will only be able to see your formatting if their e-mail client accepts Rich Text Format messages.

Emptying Your Outbox

If you're not connected to the Internet when you click the New Message window's Send button, Outlook Express places your outgoing e-mail message in its Outbox folder. To have Outlook Express pass all of the messages stored in the Outbox to your Internet service providers mail server (so that the messages can be delivered), choose the Tools menu's Send And Receive command to display the Send And Receive submenu. Then choose the command that corresponds to your Internet service provider from this submenu. Outlook Express initiates a Dial-Up Networking connection, passes your outgoing e-mail messages to the Internet service provider's mail server, and then retrieves any incoming messages from the Internet service providers mail server, too.

Retrieving Incoming E-Mail Messages

When you empty your Outbox folder following the instructions provided in the preceding paragraph, you also retrieve any incoming messages from the Internet service provider's mail server. Therefore, you retrieve incoming e-mail messages in the same manner that you deliver outgoing messages.

Reading E-Mail Messages You Receive

To read an e-mail message somebody sends you, start Outlook Express and click the Inbox icon in the **folder pane** portion of the Outlook Express window. This tells Outlook Express to list any messages people have sent you in the message list pane of the Outlook Express window.

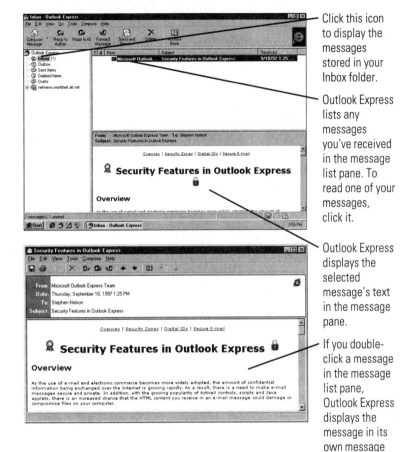

Click this icon to display the messages stored in your Inbox folder.

Outlook Express lists any messages you've received in the message list pane. To read one of your messages, click it.

Outlook Express displays the selected message's text in the message pane.

If you double-click a message in the message list pane, Outlook Express displays the message in its own message window, as shown here.

Forwarding an E-Mail Message

You can forward the open, or displayed, message to someone else by clicking the Forward Message button and then, when prompted, by specifying the e-mail address of the person you want to forward the message to.

continues

E-Mail *(continued)*

Deleting an E-Mail Message

You can delete a displayed message by clicking the Delete button. When you delete a message, Outlook Express moves the message from the Inbox folder to the Deleted Items folder.

To view the items in the Deleted Items folder, click its icon. To delete a message that shows in the Deleted items folder—this permanently deletes an item—select the item and then click the Delete button.

If you want to delete all the items shown in the Deleted Items folder, right-click the Deleted Items folder to display the shortcut menu. When Outlook Express displays the shortcut menu, choose the Empty Folder command.

Replying to E-Mail Messages

You can reply to a message by clicking the Reply To Author button. (The Reply To Author button tells Outlook Express you want to send the message to the person who created the original message.) Or you can reply to a message by sending the reply to every recipient of the original message. To do this, you click the Reply To All button.

When you reply to a message using either the Reply To Author button or the Reply To All button, Outlook Express opens a new message window, fills in the To box and Subject box for you, and copies the original message to the message text area. You can then add your reply to the message text area.

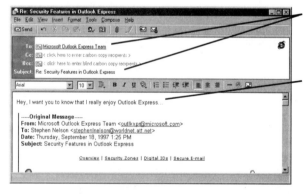

Outlook Express fills out this part of the message window for you.

Enter new message text here.

Sending Files with E-Mail Messages

Sending files with e-mail messages is known as "attaching a file." To attach a file, create a message in the usual way. Then before you click the Send button, take the following steps to attach a file to the message:

1 Click the Insert File button. Outlook Express displays the Insert Attachment dialog box.

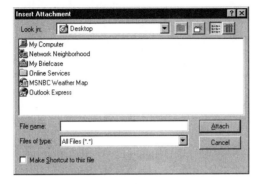

2 Use the Look In box or the Look In list box to find the folder that stores the file you want to attach.

3 When the Look In list box shows the file you want to attach, click it to select it. (After you do this, the File Name box will identify the file.)

4 Verify that the Make Shortcut To This File check box isn't checked.

5 Click the Attach button to attach the file to the message.

After you attach the file to the message, you send the message in the usual way. For example, you click the message window's Send button to place the message in your Outbox folder. Later, to deliver the messages in your Outbox folder to your Internet service provider's mail server, you'll use the Tools menu's Send And Receive command.

SEE ALSO   Digital ID; Encoded Files; Encryption

More about e-mail attachments

E-mail messages usually include just text. But they can also include binary files—such as graphics images and programs. Almost every computer user has had problems with binary e-mail attachments at one point or another. This is because the e-mail server and client programs for both the message sender and the message receiver need to recognize the same protocol. The problem is that they often don't. For instance, if someone sends you a **MIME** attachment and your Internet service provider's server or e-mail client doesn't support the MIME protocol, the attachment shows up on your screen as a bunch of indecipherable garbage. To decode this mess, you need to use a program like **WinZip** or Wincode. Just for your information, Outlook Express recognizes both MIME and **uuencode**. Contact your Internet service provider if you want to find out what protocols its server recognizes.

E-Mail Address

An e-mail address is what you use to address an e-mail message. An e-mail address is typically composed of a person's **username** and the **domain name** of their **Internet service provider.** For example, I have an **account** with The Microsoft Network (which uses the domain name *msn.com*) and my username is *stphnlnlsn*. My e-mail address is *stphnlnlsn@msn.com*.

You don't have to work with e-mail addresses if you don't want to, however. You can use the **Address Book** to make a list of people's names and e-mail addresses. And if you do record someone's name and e-mail address in your Address Book, all you need to do to address a message to them is type in their name. Outlook Express grabs the person's e-mail address from your Address Book when it's time to actually send the message.

Before we wrap up this discussion of e-mail addresses, let me mention that some people call e-mail addresses by other names. Some people call them e-mail names. And some people call them e-mail aliases.

SEE ALSO   E-Mail

E-Mail Lists SEE Mailing Lists

E-Mail Name SEE E-Mail Address

Emoticons SEE Smileys

Encoded Files

Here's one of the weird aspects of Internet **newsgroups:** You can't post binary **files,** such as **bitmap** images or programs. You can post only text. If you know much about Internet newsgroups, however, you're shaking your head now. You already know that bitmap images and programs are two of the items that people post most often.

So what gives? Well, here's the weirdness: To post a binary file—such as a picture or program—the poster first turns the binary file into a text file. Binary-to-text conversion is called encoding, or uuencoding. When someone wants to download an encoded binary file, they need to turn the text file back into a binary file. Text-to-binary conversion is called decoding, or unencoding. Fortunately, you don't need to do anything special to encode or decode binary files. Outlook Express automatically encodes binary files before you post them to newsgroups. And it automatically decodes any binary files you retrieve from newsgroups.

SEE ALSO   MIME; Uuencode

Encryption

When you encrypt something—like an e-mail message—it just means that you scramble the information so that it can't be read by anyone who doesn't know how to unscramble it. When the recipient gets your e-mail message, he or she decrypts, or unscrambles, it in order to read it.

Mechanically, encryption is pretty simple. Let's take the following message as an example:

```
I'm dating Beth's mother but don't tell Beth!
```

If I create a simple little code that, for example, substitutes the number 2 for the letter *b*, fills spaces with the letter *x*, and substitutes the dollar sign for the letter *t*, the preceding message gets encrypted into this:

```
I'mxda$ingx2e$h'sxmo$herx2u$xdon'$x$ellx2e$h!
```

See how even a simple code makes a message pretty illegible? If Beth gets or intercepts this message, she probably wouldn't stumble onto my secret. But if my intended recipient knows the encryption scheme and can apply it backwards, he or she can easily decrypt and then read my message.

Anyone who really wanted to could probably figure out my simple code in relatively short order. But with a computer you can create and use wickedly complex encryption rules. In fact, with a computer's help, you can create and use encryption rules that are practically unbreakable.

So how does all of this apply to the Internet? While encryption may seem like a subject of interest to only the paranoid and conspiracy theorists, actually it's not. Encryption is necessary for the Internet to become a truly commercial network. You wouldn't want to send your credit card number without encryption, for example. Without encryption, some miscreant might intercept your credit card number and charge a trip to Acapulco.

SEE ALSO   Digital ID; PGP; ROT13

Escape Characters

If you connect to another Internet host—perhaps you've just **telnetted** to a host—you need a way to disconnect when you're finished. The way you disconnect is by pressing an escape character. The escape character is probably a two-character key sequence that you type to signal you want to disconnect.

When you connect to the U.S. Library of Congress's telnet site, for example, you're told, among other things, that the escape character is ^]. The caret symbol (^) signifies the Ctrl key. So to disconnect from the Library of Congress's telnet site, you press Ctrl+].

Typically, you get a lot of information when you first connect to a host, and buried in that information is the escape character. Be sure to write it down. Or failing that, try some of the more common escape sequences—such as Ctrl+] or Ctrl+C.

Want to telnet to the Library of Congress?

To telnet to the Library of Congress, you just need to enter the full **uniform resource locator** (URL) for the Library of Congress's telnet site in the Internet Explorer Address box. The full URL is *telnet://locis.loc.gov*. When you enter the telnet URL, Internet Explorer starts the Windows telnet client, which is what you'll use to work with the Library of Congress web site. By the way, once you connect to the Library of Congress or to any other telnet site, you use the site's menus to navigate and use the system.

Ethernet

Ethernet is a hardware standard for **LANs** developed by Xerox. It is one of the most popular standards. Ethernet can transfer data at speeds up to 10Mbps. So that's pretty cool. (You do need to have an Ethernet adapter for your PC to connect to an Ethernet-based LAN.) This digression into network topology may seem irrelevant to a discussion of the Internet. But it is important to note that because Ethernet is so much faster than most of the connections the Internet uses, many of the things that people do on the Internet work even better on an **intranet** running a company's LAN.

Let me see if there's anything else I can say about Ethernet... as long as we're on the subject, I may as well tell you that there are three ways to make the actual connection based on the adapter and network: thin Ethernet cable using a BNC connector, twisted pair or 10BASE-T cable using an RJ-45 connector, and Thick Ethernet cable using an AUI connector.

Oh, one other thing. Although Ethernet is pretty fast, its **bandwidth** is not fast enough for future multimedia applications. For that reason, a new protocol called Fast Ethernet is under development that will allow speeds up to 100Mbps.

SEE ALSO   Bits Per Second

Exchange

You use Microsoft Exchange to send and read **e-mail** messages if you've made a **PPP** connection to the Internet. However, this book assumes you'll want to use Outlook Express rather than Exchange because Outlook Express comes with Internet Explorer.

Explorer Bar

The Explorer bar is a portion on the left side of the Internet Explorer window that shows a list of **hyperlinks** you can click. In the right portion of the window, Internet Explorer shows the active **web page**. By clicking the hyperlinks in the Explorer bar, you change the web page shown in the right portion of the Internet Explorer window.

To display the Explorer bar, choose the View menu's Explorer bar command. You can also display the Explorer bar by clicking the Search, **Favorites,** History, or **Channels** buttons. After Internet Explorer displays the Explorer bar, click some of the hyperlinks to see how the open web page changes.

continues

Explorer Bar *(continued)*

This is the Explorer bar.

When you click a hyperlink in the Explorer bar, this portion of the Internet Explorer window shows the web page that the hyperlink points to.

You can change the size of the Explorer bar by dragging this border.

FAQ

FAQ is an acronym for Frequently Asked Questions. A FAQ is a compilation of questions and answers posted often on **newsgroups** and **mailing lists.** FAQs do a couple of things. They give you a feel for what a newsgroup or mailing list is about, and they keep questions that have already been answered many times from appearing yet again.

You probably should read the FAQ for a newsgroup or mailing list you're interested in. Unless you're someone who enjoys being the subject of nasty criticism and endless **flames,** you should definitely check a group's FAQ before you post.

Just the FAQs, ma'am

FAQs are posted regularly in newsgroups as well as on *news://news.answers.* Archives of almost all FAQs can be found at *ftp://rtfm.mit.edu/pub/usenet.* A good search form can be found at *http://www.cis.ohio-state.edu/hypertext/faq/usenet/top.html.*

SEE ALSO Netiquette

Favorites

Favorites is the name of a folder that lists **web pages** you've said are so cool that you want Internet Explorer to memorize their **uniform resource locators** (URLs). You can guess why Internet Explorer lets you do this. By memorizing a URL, you don't have to remember some lengthy, complicated URL when you want to visit the web site again.

Adding an Item to Your Favorites List

To add the current web page to your favorites list, choose the Favorites menu's Add To Favorites command. When Internet Explorer displays the Add Favorite dialog box, name the favorite and click OK.

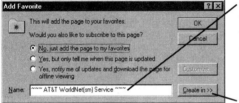

Internet Explorer suggests you use the web page name to identify the favorite, but you'll sometimes want to change this to something more descriptive.

If you want to store the favorite in one of the Favorite folder's subfolders, click the Create In button.

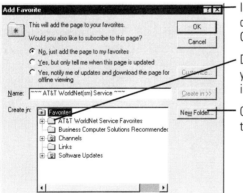

Internet Explorer displays this dialog box after you click the Create In button.

Double-click the subfolder you want to store the favorite in.

Click the New Folder button to create a new subfolder.

continues

Favorites *(continued)*

Visiting a Favorite Web Page

To visit a favorite web page, you use the Favorites menu commands or the Favorites button.

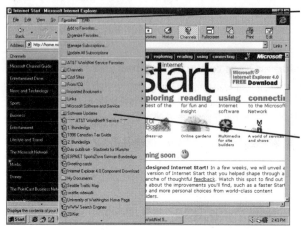

If you've stored the favorite web page's URL in the Favorites folder, you choose the web page from the Favorites menu.

If you stored the favorite web page in a subfolder of the Favorites folder, click the subfolder and then choose the web page from the subfolder.

File

In Computerland, you work with files. Data gets stored in files. Applications, or programs, are stored in files. When you begin work, you open a file. When you're finished, you save and close it.

One of the main tasks the Internet performs, of course, is moving these files around. And, in fact, there's a protocol you'll probably work with that was created for the express purpose of moving files between Internet hosts: FTP.

File Extensions

Windows appends a three-letter file extension at the end of filenames to identify the file type. Because Windows does this, many of the files you download from the Internet also use a file extension to identify the file type.

What's more, because so many Internet users are also Windows users, it's considered good manners to **upload** files that follow the Windows file-naming conventions and use the three-letter file extension. Just so you know what some of the file extensions identify, I've listed the common ones in the table that follows:

File extension	Type of file
ARC	A compressed file that's been scrunched with the archive utility.
EXE	A program, or executable, file.
GIF	A **bitmap** file that uses the Graphics Interchange Format, or **GIF.**
JPG	A bitmap file that uses the Joint Photographic Experts Group, or **JPEG,** format.
MPG	A video that uses the Moving Pictures Experts Group, or **MPEG,** format.
TXT	A text file.
UUE	A binary file—such as a program or bitmap file—that's been turned into text using a uuencode utility. To turn this file back into a program or bitmap file, you'll need to decode, or unencode, it.
ZIP	A file that's been compressed, or scrunched, using the **PKZIP** or **WinZip** utility.

Filenames

With the newest versions of Windows—which Internet Explorer uses—you don't really have to worry about file-naming rules. For all practical purposes, you can use as many characters as you want in a filename. But things are a bit different on the Internet. Because of the legacy of MS-DOS's file-naming limitations and conventions (MS-DOS limited filenames to eight characters), you should limit the names of the files you upload to eight characters. All numbers and letters that appear on your keyboard are okay to use in filenames. And so are many other characters. You shouldn't, however, use characters that MS-DOS expects to use in special ways on its command line. These forbidden characters include spaces, asterisks, and question marks.

Filenames *(continued)*

Naming a file

You usually give a file its filename when you choose the application's File Save As command. For example, if you want to save a copy of the web page shown in the Internet Explorer window, you choose the File menu's Save As command. The Save As dialog box includes a box you use to name the file.

File Pane

When you start **Windows Explorer,** Windows displays a document window that shows the stuff that's connected to your computer—including any **folders** and **files.** This window is split into two portions that I'm calling panes.

Since the right pane is the only one that shows files, I decided to call it the file pane. I should say that this is just something I made up. I don't think you'll see this term any place else, but if you do, tell them "Steve Nelson was here."

SEE ALSO   My Computer

Finger

People with **shell accounts** usually have a special command available, called finger. (To be precise, this command is actually a **client** that runs on the **Internet service provider's** computer.) Here's the scoop. If you know someone's **e-mail address** and the **domain name** of the host they use, you might be able to learn their true identity by "fingering" them. For example, say you've just gotten a message from someone named "nelson" at uxx.edu. Perhaps, before you reply, you want to learn a bit more about this person. So you finger them. To do this, type the command finger at the command prompt, followed by the person's e-mail address. For example, to learn the true identify of *nelson@uxx.edu,* you would type:

```
finger nelson@uxx.edu
```

Assuming the host you've fingered responds (and it may not), what you'll see next is some information on the certain someone you fingered, such as that shown here:

```
[uxx.edu]
        Name:  Nelson, Peter C.
  Department:  Electrical Engineering
       Title:  Associate Professor
       Phone:  555-3210
         Fax:  555-1234
     Address:  3015 ERF
           :  Campus MC 154
   E-mail to:  Peter.C.Nelson@uxx.edu
 ADN Account:  nelson@xxx.uxx.edu
```

Flame

A flame is an **e-mail** message that's mean and nasty. If you e-mail a message to me and say that I'm a complete moron, utterly incapable of constructing a sentence, for example, that's a flame. By the way, if I e-mail you back a message that says your mother wears army boots and your sister is ugly, what we've got going is a "flame war."

Flames, as you might guess, violate all the rules of Internet good manners and etiquette. But because some of the people out surfing the Internet have the maturity of grade schoolers, you'll see quite a few flames. On a philosophical note, I suspect that the anonymity of the Internet has something to do with this meanness. You can say something really mean and threatening on the Internet, but you don't have to see the person's face or run into them at the grocery store.

SEE ALSO   Netiquette; Spam

Folder

Windows uses folders to organize your disks and the **files** they store. (Folders, by the way, replace MS-DOS's directories.) You can also organize the files in a folder by creating folders within a folder. Basically, folders work like the drawers in a filing cabinet. You can create folders and see how your disk is organized into folders by using **Windows Explorer**.

SEE ALSO   Subfolder

Folder Pane

I'm using the term *folder pane* to refer to the left portion of the window that Windows Explorer displays to show you what's connected to your computer, how your disks' folders are organized, and which files are in the active folder.

Frame

Smart web browsers like **Internet Explorer** and **Netscape Navigator** let you break their browser windows into chunks called frames. Frames are neat because they let you view different **web pages** at the same time.

Freenet

The term *freenet* refers to an Internet **host** that people can use for free and thereby connect to the Internet for free. Schools, community groups, and libraries are often providers of freenet sites. If you're interested in exploring this angle, you might want to make telephone calls to schools, community groups, and libraries in your town.

On the subject of freenet sites, the downtown public library where I live (Seattle) provides a freenet site, and it has become popular with a bunch of homeless men. These guys, who call themselves the "network geeks," spend their considerable free time surfing the Internet from the library's freenet site. As one of the network geeks explained, "Hey, we're homeless, not stupid."

Free Speech

You bought this book to learn more about the mechanics of Internet Explorer and the technology of the Internet. I know that. But I want to digress for just a moment and talk about free speech and the Internet.

The Internet, as you might know, makes it possible to share one's thoughts and ideas with millions of people. While this power isn't all that remarkable—after all, television and some of the big newspapers do it on a daily basis—it is remarkable in that there's no obligatory censorship or filtering of the information.

Think about it for a minute. Nowhere else can someone share a thought or idea with millions of people freely, without the help of editors, journalists, and media executives. That's the "good news," so to speak. But there's a "bad news" element to this lack of informal censorship and filtering. And it's the flip side of the same coin. Someone—anyone with an Internet connection—can share a thought or idea with millions of people freely. And in any group of 20 million people, of course, you'll find a few goofballs, dingbats, and dirtbags.

I strongly believe the good news outweighs the bad news. But I need to warn you: because some editor or journalist isn't filtering information for you, you need to filter the information for yourself. And because the Internet community is culturally diverse, you will most assuredly find material you disagree with on any subject about which you feel strongly. Politics. Religion. Sexuality. Good grammar.

I'm not going to spend any more space on this. But I encourage you to respect and appreciate the enormous benefits of the Internet's contribution to free speech.

Bad news for filmmakers, novelists, and conspiracy theorists

Jeepers, because we're on the subject, I should also mention that this communication change is bad news for some filmmakers, novelists, and conspiracy theorists. A fundamental element of many thriller stories and conspiracy theories is a protagonist who has vital information but can't share it with anybody important. Note, however, that with the Internet, this idea is totally outdated. In fact, by my rough calculation, more than a few of Alfred Hitchcock's movies, some of Robert Ludlum's novels, and most conspiracy theories become impossibly farfetched in light of this radical change in communication. If you have hard evidence that some world leader is a criminal, for example, you can post the evidence to an Internet **newsgroup** today and probably topple a government tomorrow. If you discover a cheap, renewable, safe energy source some Friday afternoon, you can tell the world about it over the weekend, and no one—not even somebody or some organization with billions or trillions of dollars to lose—can stop you.

FrontPage Express

Microsoft FrontPage Express amounts to a "lite" version of Microsoft FrontPage Editor, which is part of the Microsoft FrontPage suite of web-publishing programs. What FrontPage Express lets you do is create HTML documents (without actually knowing **HTML**) so that you can publish them on the Internet or an **intranet.** If you're interested in becoming a **web publisher,** go ahead and experiment with FrontPage Express. If you're familiar with other Microsoft programs (and in particular Microsoft Word), you'll soon be creating attractive web pages.

FTP

FTP is an acronym for file transfer protocol. FTP allows you to move **files** from one Internet **host** to another. In fact, some hosts are set up specifically so you can rummage around inside them and look for stuff to FTP back to your host. (Your host can be either your Internet service provider's computer or your own PC.) These hosts are called, not surprisingly, FTP sites. If any Joe or Jane can log on to an FTP site—and there are plenty of sites they can log on to—the FTP site is called an **anonymous FTP** site.

FTPing with Internet Explorer

Internet Explorer makes it very easy to move files from an FTP site to your computer. All you have to do is enter the ftp site's **uniform resource locator** (URL) in the Address box. When you do, Internet Explorer displays the contents of the site's root directory, or root folder.

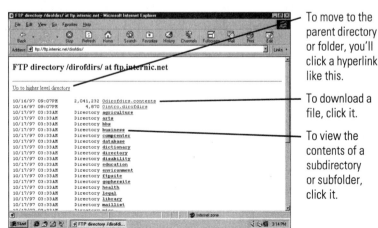

To move to the parent directory or folder, you'll click a hyperlink like this.

To download a file, click it.

To view the contents of a subdirectory or subfolder, click it.

Starting an FTP Session so You Can Use the FTP Client

Windows comes with an FTP client. Although if you just want to download files from an FTP site, there's no reason to use this tool. As noted in the preceding paragraphs, you can download files from an FTP site using Internet Explorer. However, if you want to perform other FTP operations—say you want to upload a file to an FTP site—you need to use the Windows FTP client. Your first step, should you want to do this, is to start an FTP session.

To start an FTP session, first start the FTP **client** and then follow these steps:

1 Start **Windows Explorer** by clicking the Start button and then choosing Programs and Windows Explorer.

2 Display the contents of the Windows **folder.** (Depending on how your system is set up, the folder may be named something other than "Windows." In that case, just substitute the correct name in the following instructions.) One way to do this is by scrolling through the **folder pane** and then double-clicking on the Windows folder.

3 Open the FTP program. One way to do this is by scrolling through the **file pane** and then double-clicking on the FTP program. Once you've opened the FTP program, you'll see the FTP window in the middle of the Windows **desktop.**

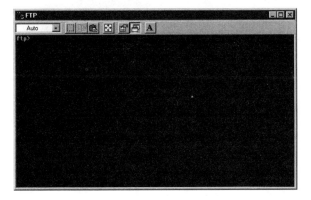

If you FTP often...

If you FTP often, set up a **shortcut icon** for the FTP program. A shortcut icon makes it much easier to start the FTP client. With a shortcut icon—it will appear on the **desktop**—all you do is double-click the icon to start the FTP client.

continues

FTP *(continued)*

Connecting to an FTP Site with Windows 95's FTP Client

To connect to an FTP site, type the command *open* followed by the name of the FTP site. For example, to connect to the anonymous FTP site ftp.microsoft.com, type *open ftp.microsoft.com*. (If you've not already made your PPP or SLIP connection, Windows will start **Dial-Up Networking** as soon as you try to connect to another host. Note that you don't need to make a Dial-Up Networking connection if you're already connected to the Internet.) Once you connect, you'll be prompted for your username and a password.

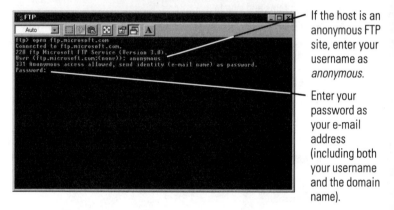

If the host is an anonymous FTP site, enter your username as *anonymous*.

Enter your password as your e-mail address (including both your username and the domain name).

Retrieving Files with the Windows FTP Client

Finding files using FTP is tough. In fact, it's mainly for this reason that Internet tools such as **Archie** were developed. If you don't know what you're looking for, try using Archie.

Once you do find the file you're looking for, it's easy to retrieve it. Just type the *get* command followed by the filename. The FTP client will move the file from the FTP site to your host. For example, to retrieve a file named disclaimer.txt at *ftp.microsoft.com,* you would type the following:

```
get disclaimer.txt
```

Disconnecting from an FTP Site with the Windows FTP Client

To disconnect from an FTP site, type the command *disconnect* at the command prompt. You'll see some messages, including one that says you've disconnected. If you want to connect to another FTP site, you can. Just follow the instructions in the paragraph at the top of this page about connecting to an FTP site with Windows's FTP client. If you want to end the FTP session, type the command *quit*.

SEE ALSO   Gopher; Internet Explorer; Troubleshooting: FTP; Quick Reference: FTP Client Commands

Full Screen

To see more of a web page on your screen at once, you can view the web page as a full screen. Click the Fullscreen button on the toolbar to toggle in and out of the full screen mode.

When you display a web page as a full screen, the menu bar and the Windows Taskbar disappear.

Gateway

A gateway is just a computer that connects an **IP** network and a non-IP network. For example, **online services** such as **America Online,** CompuServe, The **Microsoft Network,** and Prodigy use gateways to connect to the Internet.

SEE ALSO   Bridge; Outernet

GIF

A GIF file is a bitmap file that uses the Graphics Interchange Format (GIF) file format. There's an ongoing argument about whether GIF files look better than the usual substitute, **JPEG** files. Some people swear that GIFs look better and that anyone who uploads anything else is either a simpleton or a jerk. The truth, however, is that high-quality JPEG files look just as good as high-quality GIF files to the naked eye. What's more, JPEG files are smaller and, therefore, a lot quicker to upload and download. To look at a GIF file, you need to have a viewer such as **Internet Explorer.**

SEE ALSO   Downloading Files

Gigabyte

A gigabyte is roughly 1000 **megabytes.** Since a megabyte is roughly 1000 **kilobytes,** it follows that a gigabyte is roughly 1,000,000 kilobytes. That's big. Really big. For example, with a 28.8Kbps **modem** spewing data at a rate of 28.8Kbps, it would probably take three or four days to download a gigabyte of stuff.

Nits on bits

In the preceding paragraph, I gave only rough descriptions of the terms *megabyte* and *gigabyte*. To be painstakingly precise, a megabyte is actually 1024 kilobytes, and a gigabyte is actually 1024 megabytes or 1,048,576 kilobytes.

Gopher

The great thing about the Internet is all the information it provides, but there's a problem with this. You need a way to sift through everything. You need a way to find the specific piece of data you want. You need, well, you need Gopher.

What's Gopher? Gopher is, in essence, a menu of Internet **resources.** These menus are maintained by Gopher servers. (The stuff that appears on Gopher menus is collectively called "Gopherspace.")

Understanding Gopher

To use Gopher, you just connect to a Gopher **server.** Then you begin choosing menu options. Ideally, you narrow the range of topics as you choose menu options, and then you find the topic you want.

Typically, Gopher servers emphasize a particular information category. Agricultural research. Federal law. Stuff like that. No matter which Gopher server you connect to, some of the menu options you see are, in essence, connections to other Gopher servers.

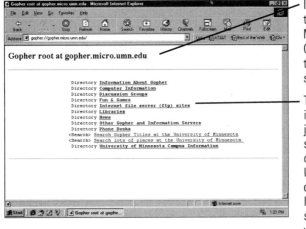

If I connect to the University of Minnesota Gopher server, this is what I see.

To search for information, I just start selecting menu options. Ultimately, I will connect to an Internet **resource** such as a **file** you can **FTP** or a **telnet** site.

Connecting to a Gopher

To connect to a Gopher server, all you need to do is start Internet Explorer and then enter the **uniform resource locator** (URL) for a Gopher server in the Address box. (If this is a Gopher server that you'll want to connect to frequently, you may want to add the URL to your **favorites** list.)

Using Gopher

Once you've connected to a Gopher server, you start choosing menu options. If you connect to a Gopher server that itself catalogs information of the kind you're looking for, you may be able to find what you're looking for rather quickly. (Keep your fingers crossed.)

Once you find that bit of information you're interested in, you can select it by clicking the resource. Gopher downloads the file to your computer. If Internet Explorer knows which application opens the file, it will even open the file for you. (In the case of text files, Internet Explorer displays the text file itself.)

Finding Resources with Searchable Indexes

To make it easier to find resources, Gopher provides three search tools: searchable indexes, Veronica, and Jughead. I'll describe searchable indexes first. In the next two sections, I'll describe how to use Veronica and Jughead.

continues

Gopher *(continued)*

Okay, here's the deal on searchable indexes. Some of the menu options Gopher presents aren't really menu options, or not in the regular sense. They let you tell the Gopher server that you want to search through the resources it catalogs. When you choose one of these menu options, called searchable indexes, Gopher displays a dialog box. To use the searchable index, you enter a keyword or a couple of keywords that describe the subject you're interested in and then press the Enter key. The Gopher server then builds a list of resources that use the keyword or keywords you specified.

Finding Resources with Veronica

If you think about it for a minute, there's a problem with searchable indexes. They only look at an index of stuff for a Gopher directory. That means if you want to look in a lot of different places, you have to search a lot of searchable indexes. So how do you find the Gopher server or directory in the first place? You use Veronica. Veronica searches Gopher servers and Gopher directories. If it can find a server or directory associated with a keyword or keywords that you specify in your search, it lets you know.

Mechanically, using Veronica is like using a regular old searchable index. The only difference is that rather than choosing a Gopher menu option that describes itself as a search index or an index, you choose a Gopher menu option that's named "Search Gopherspace Using Veronica," or something like that. Usually, you see a menu option that references Veronica on the main menu for a Gopher server.

1 Start Internet Explorer, and if necessary, connect to the Internet in the usual way.

2 Connect to a Gopher server by entering its URL in the Address box.

3 Choose the Gopher menu option that references Veronica. You may get another menu of options that let you choose the specific Gopher server that will perform the Veronica search or the type of Veronica search: server names, directory names, and so on. If you do, choose one of these options.

4 When prompted, enter the keyword (or keywords) you want to use to search "Gopherspace."

5 Initiate the search by pressing the Enter key.

Once Gopher finishes its search, it displays a list of Gopher servers, directories, or menu options that match your keyword. You can then move to a server, directory, or menu option by selecting it.

Veronica is smart

I haven't described Veronica's search capabilities in much detail here. But you should know that Veronica lets you get quite sophisticated about the way you specify search criteria. You can use Boolean logic, for example. If you're interested in these kinds of advanced search techniques, keep your eyes open for a **FAQ** about Veronica. It will probably appear as another menu option near the menu option that lets you search "Gopherspace" using Veronica.

Finding Resources with Jughead

Jughead is another search tool. Jughead works sort of like Veronica and sort of like a searchable index. In effect, what Jughead searches is a searchable index of a group of Gopher servers. Note that you won't always see the name "Jughead" on a menu. Instead, you'll sometimes see a menu option named something like "Search Gopher Titles at the University of Minnesota."

Gulf War

One of the interesting features of the Internet is that the information that gets passed around is broken into little chunks called **packets.** It's these little packets that get passed from the sending **network** to the receiving network. Different packets may actually travel different routes on the network and arrive at the receiving network in a different order. But because the Internet is set up to deal with these packets, nothing gets jumbled or lost. If a packet does get lost somewhere in route, no trouble—the system is smart enough to notice the missing packet and have it sent again. The TCP/IP protocol creates, tracks, and reassembles the packets.

Okay. I know this entry says "Gulf War." And you're wondering what any of this has to do with Iraq, Sadaam Hussein, Kuwait, or George Bush. But there is a connection. TCP/IP protocol exists because roughly three decades ago the United States government needed to create a network that wouldn't get knocked out in, say, a thermonuclear exchange with the former Soviet Union. For example, if a big Internet host in, say, Chicago, got wiped out, the network needed to automatically recover and then start routing stuff through St. Louis, or Minneapolis, or wherever. The U.S., fortunately, never got a chance to test the network in a real-life setting. But, unfortunately, the Iraqis did during the Gulf War. The verdict? The rumor mill says that despite the best efforts of Norman Schwarzkopf and crew, the allies either never did shut down or had a terrible time shutting down the computer network that the Iraqis relied on for their command and control activities. And the reason the allies had so much trouble cutting Iraqi communications was because of this TCP/IP protocol stuff.

SEE ALSO   Packet-Switching Network

Home Page

The term *home page* is a bit nebulous. Sometimes people use the phrase to refer to the **start page** you see when you first start Internet Explorer. Other times, people use the term to refer to a personal web page (perhaps showing pictures of your family) that they've set up to provide personal or business information.

SEE ALSO   FrontPage Express

Host Computer

A host computer is just a computer that's connected to the Internet. For example, if you connect your PC to the Internet using a **PPP** connection, your PC temporarily becomes a host computer. Of course, any of the mainframe computers or minicomputers that you connect to are also host computers.

I'm not all that fussy a person. Really. But I will be picky and tell you that if you've connected to an **Internet service provider** using a **shell account** and a communications application like **HyperTerminal,** your computer isn't actually a host computer. You're connected to a host computer that's part of the Internet.

SEE ALSO   Server

Host Names

Host names provide an easy way to identify hosts so you don't have to remember a host's **IP** number. Each host name can correspond to only one IP number. Host addresses have the format *hostname.domainname*—for example, *ftp.microsoft.com.* In this case, *ftp* is the host name and *microsoft.com* is the domain name. **DNS** (Domain Name Service), by the way, does the mapping of host names to IP numbers.

Hot Link

A hot link is what you click in a **World Wide Web** document to move from document to document. Hot links are also called **hyperlinks,** hypertext links, and **anchors.**

HTML

The acronym HTML stands for Hypertext Markup Language. HTML is what you use to create **World Wide Web** documents. In fact, for this reason, the HTML acronym is often used as the last part of a World Wide Web document name—to identify what it is. (On PCs, World Wide Web documents use the **file extension** HTM for the same basic reason.) Do you need to know this? No, not really. The only time you'd even need to worry about or work with HTML is if you were creating your own World Wide Web documents.

SEE ALSO   FrontPage Express

HTTP

This acronym stands for Hypertext Transfer Protocol. HTTP is the **protocol** that makes the **World Wide Web** possible. You may actually want to remember this acronym, because officially the **uniform resource locator** (URL) for every World Wide Web site starts with it. For example, the Microsoft Corporation's World Wide Web site looks like this:

```
http://www.microsoft.com
```

Note, however, that most web browsers, including Internet Explorer, don't require you to include the http:// part of a web page's URL. If you leave off this prefix, the web browser assumes it should use the prefix.

Hyperlink

Hyperlinks are those clickable chunks of text and clickable pictures you use to move to another web page. In other words, basically they're just **uniform resource locators** (URLs). The URL doesn't show up of course. It's hidden. Instead you see text or a picture that (hopefully) describes or identifies what the URL points to.

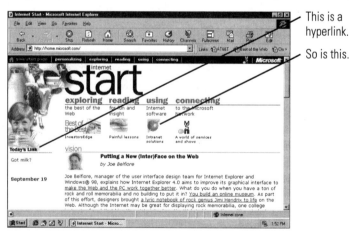

This is a hyperlink.

So is this.

I should mention that not all hyperlinks point to web pages. Some start your e-mail client (probably Outlook Express) so that you can send a message to the person who's **e-mail address** is described in the hyperlink. And some hyperlinks point to resources that aren't part of the World Wide Web but that are part of the Internet, such as **FTP** sites, **Gopher** servers, and **telnet** sites. When a hyperlink points to a resource that isn't part of the World Wide Web, clicking the hyperlink typically starts another Internet client.

HyperTerminal

HyperTerminal is Windows's powerful communications application. With it and a **modem,** you can connect your computer to another computer, to an electronic mail service, and to many electronic bulletin board systems, or BBSs. If you connect to the Internet using an Internet service provider and you're using a **shell account** and not making a PPP or SLIP connection, for example, you probably use HyperTerminal. Because this book doesn't talk about shell accounts and instead assumes you're making a **Dial-Up Networking** connection so that you can use Internet Explorer, I won't say more about HyperTerminal. But if you have questions, refer to the Windows documentation.

Inbox Assistant

The Inbox Assistant is a feature of **Outlook Express.** What it does is let you specify rules that Outlook Express should apply when messages appear in your Inbox folder. For example, you can use the Inbox Assistant to automatically remove messages that use specified words in their subject descriptions. And you can use the Inbox Assistant to automatically forward, delete, or reply to messages that come from certain people.

SEE ALSO   E-Mail

Infoseek SEE Search Engine

Installing Internet Explorer

It's very easy to install Internet Explorer. But the way you install Internet Explorer and the options available differ depending on how you got the Internet Explorer program and any related programs.

Installing Internet Explorer from Microsoft's Web Site

It's very possible (although I can't say for sure) that Microsoft will make available a free version of its Internet Explorer program on its web site. If you get Internet Explorer in this way, you need to follow whatever instructions the web site provides.

Installing Internet Explorer from CD or Disk

If you purchased or received Internet Explorer on a CD or disk, you install Internet Explorer in the same way that you install other programs. To do this, follow these steps:

1 Click the Start button, click Settings, and then click Control Panel. Windows displays the Control Panel window.

2 Double-click the Add/Remove Programs tool.

3 Click the Install button, and then follow the on-screen instructions.

About Your Installation Options

If you have the complete Internet Explorer suite of programs (say because you purchased Internet Explorer at the local software store), you will probably have a choice as to the Internet Explorer programs you can install. You can perform a "browser-only" installation, which installs only the Internet Explorer web browser client and some peripheral multimedia enhancements. You can perform a standard installation, which adds Outlook Express to the browser-only installation. And you can perform a full installation, which adds several other Internet clients (such as Microsoft Chat and Microsoft NetMeeting) as well as handy tools for web publishing (such as Microsoft FrontPage Express and Web Publishing Wizard) to the standard installation.

Integrated Service Digital Network SEE ISDN

Internet Address

When common folk like you and me use the term *Internet address,* we probably mean the **username** and **domain name** that are used to e-mail someone. If you want to e-mail the President of the United States, for example, you can use this address:

```
president@whitehouse.gov
```

The *president* part of the address is the person's name (or in this case, the person's title). The *whitehouse.gov* part of the address is the domain name. This makes sense, right? (By the way, if you want to talk the talk, you describe this address as "president at Whitehouse dot gov." The @ symbol is called "at.")

Some people, I should tell you, use the term Internet addresses to mean the same thing as **IP addresses,** or Internet Protocol addresses. IP addresses are the numbers that identify a specific host and domain. We could talk about IP addresses, but let's not. Unless you're setting up a **PPP** or **SLIP** connection manually, you'll never encounter them. And even then, you'll only have to noodle around with them once.

SEE ALSO   DNS; E-Mail Address; Host Names

Internet Call SEE NetMeeting

Internet Explorer

Internet Explorer is Microsoft's web browser—and the principal subject of this Field Guide. As described in other A to Z entries, you use the Internet Explorer for **web browsing,** to FTP, and with **Gopher.**

SEE ALSO   Quick Reference: Internet Explorer Commands *and* Internet Explorer Toolbar Guide

Internet Service Provider

An Internet service provider, or ISP, is a company that lets you connect to its Internet host, usually for a fee. Once you're connected, your computer works either like a temporary Internet host or like a "dumb terminal" on which you can use the Internet by means of your connection to the provider's network. (When your computer works like a dumb terminal, you use your keyboard and your monitor, but it's really the other computer and its software that you're using.) People who talk about the Internet being an "information superhighway" like to say that Internet service providers are like on-ramps—they give you a way to get on the road.

One point that's a little bit confusing but important to understand is that you pay an Internet service provider merely to *access* the Internet. You're not paying anything to *use* the Internet. To go back to the on-ramps on the information superhighway analogy, Internet service providers set up tollbooths on the on-ramps that you must go through before you can get on the highway. But you actually use the highway for free.

Let me give you a few tips on picking an Internet service provider. First, check prices. You can pay anywhere from $10 to around $50 a month for an Internet service provider's service. (To keep your costs down, you'll probably want to choose a local provider—to save on long-distance telephone charges.) Second, you should verify that you'll be able to connect when you want. (You can test this just by trying to connect a few times before you actually sign up.) Finally, you probably want to verify that your Internet service provider gives you access to the **resources** that interest you. (Some Internet service providers don't give you access to the more controversial and sensational newsgroups, for example.) So ask about access to whatever you're interested in.

SEE ALSO   Connections; Outernet; Shell Account

Internet Society

The Internet Society is an international organization that coordinates the Internet and its technologies and applications. You can find more information about the Internet Society at the **World Wide Web** site *http://www.isoc.org.*

InterNIC

InterNIC refers to the Internet Network Information Center. The InterNIC stores information about the Internet. The InterNIC, for example, has information about all the various Internet standards that define and describe the **network** itself. The InterNIC also has information about a bunch of FTP sites. Its **uniform resource locator** is *ftp.internic.net.*

Intranet

An intranet is just an internal, private **network** that uses the **TCP/IP** protocol. (Many large organizations maintain intranets, for example.) You can use Internet Explorer to browse the **web pages** on an intranet in the exact same manner as you use it to browse web pages on the Internet.

IP

IP is an acronym for Internet Protocol. It is the network layer in the TCP/IP protocol. It ensures that **packets** get delivered to the correct destinations. IP is also the protocol after which the Internet was named.

IP Address

The IP address is the numeric address of a **host computer.** As a practical matter, you never need to worry about IP addresses unless you're involved in manually setting up a **PPP** or **SLIP** connection. Typically, the **Connection Wizard** automatically sets up your PPP or SLIP connection.

SEE ALSO   DNS; E-Mail Address

ISDN

ISDN, the acronym for Integrated Services Digital Network, amounts to a super-fast telephone line you can use to connect to the Internet. While the fastest **modems** move data at 56.6 kilobits per second, for example, ISDN moves data at 128 kilobits per second. To make an ISDN connection, you need a special ISDN modem and ISDN service from your phone company. Your **Internet service provider** must also support ISDN connections.

ISP SEE **Internet Service Provider**

Java

Java is a programming language. This means that it actually isn't all that relevant to people who just want to use the Internet as a tool. However, you'll see the term used in quite a few places because Java lets **web publishers** write programs that can run on different computers. For example, a web publisher can write a Java program that calculates loan payments. (Perhaps the web publisher is a mortgage company using its web site to attract new borrowers.) And in this scenario, people viewing the web page with different computers can use the Java loan payment program to calculate their loan payments. Or at least they can as long as their web browsers know Java. If you're using a Windows personal computer and your web browser knows Java, you'll be able to run the program. If I'm using an Apple Macintosh and my web browser knows Java, I'll be able to run the program. If someone else is using a big computer and a Java-aware web browser, he'll also be able to run the Java program.

JPEG

JPEG is a graphics file format. (The name is actually an acronym for Joint Photographic Experts Group.) Basically, the JPEG file format was created because people felt that other graphics file formats, including the ever-popular **GIF** format, were too big. Some people think that JPEG is inferior to GIF. But high-quality JPEGs, to most people's eyes, look just as good as high-quality GIFs. And they're typically significantly smaller. You can identify JPEG files because they have the letters JPG as their **file extensions.**

Viewing JPEG Images

To view a JPEG file, you'll either need a browser with an internal JPEG viewer—like Internet Explorer—or an external viewer. Any viewer deserving of the name, however, will let you view JPEG files.

How JPEG Compression Works

To compress graphics images, the JPEG format simplifies an image by using fewer colors. And this is what reduces the image's size. While this of course does reduce the quality of the image—it usually doesn't reduce the quality of the image on your computer screen. What JPEG does is take two colors that are quite similar—say a very pale yellow-green and a very, very pale yellow-green—and make them both the same color (perhaps just a very pale yellow-green).

One challenge and potential problem with JPEG images, however, is that the image's creator typically gets to specify the degree of image compression that the final JPEG image uses. (The image creator does this in a graphics or illustration program.) If the image creator forces a lot of image compression, the color simplification can end up going too far. For example, the graphics program used to create the compressed JPEG image may be forced to treat colors that aren't all that similar—say a very pale yellow-green and a pale green—as equivalent, even though they won't be equivalent to most people's eyes. When this occurs, a JPEG image does suffer.

Kilobit

A kilobit is 1024 **bits.** You will find this information relevant because modem speeds are usually measured in kilobits. Don't confuse the terms *kilobit* and *kilobyte.* It takes eight kilobits to make one kilobyte.

Kilobyte

I know you didn't buy this book to learn about the guts of your computer. But since I've used the term *kilobyte* in a couple of places, I thought I should at least define it. A byte is an eight-digit string of 1s and 0s that your computer uses to represent a character. (These 1s and 0s are called **bits.**) This, for example, is a byte:

01010100

A kilobyte is roughly 1000 of these bytes. (Or to be excruciatingly precise, a kilobyte is exactly 1024 of these bytes.)

SEE ALSO   Megabyte

LAN

LAN is an acronym for local area **network**. A LAN, for example, might connect all the computers in an office or in a building. You hear this term a lot in discussions about the Internet and about **intranets.** I don't know why. Whether an Internet **host** is on a LAN, a **MAN**, or a **WAN** makes little difference.

LISTSERV

LISTSERV is one of the more popular **mailing list** manager programs. (The other two mailing list programs you often see are Listproc and Majordomo.) So what does a mailing list manager program do? Simple. It adds users to and removes users from a mailing list. You can tell whether LISTSERV is the program used to maintain a particular mailing list because the **e-mail** address to which you send your subscription and termination requests will have LISTSERV in its name.

Log On

Logging on is what you do to connect to an Internet **host.** Specifically, logging on means to give your **username** and a **password** when you start using a computer.

Lurk

As far as your neighbor's rhododendron beds go, lurking is a bad thing. Especially if done at night. You don't want to lurk. You may get arrested.

In a **newsgroup** or **mailing list,** however, lurking is good. It means to quietly observe. It means to read the posted messages and get a feel for what goes on and what doesn't before posting a message yourself. By lurking, you won't post a stupid message and get **flamed.**

Lycos SEE Search Engine

Mailing List

On the Internet, a mailing list is just a list of people who want to receive information via e-mail about a particular topic: BMW motorcycles, a particular television show, or some quirky author. If you want to receive information about a particular topic covered by a mailing list, you ask the mailing list administrator to have your name added to the mailing list. If you have something relevant to say about a topic, you can **e-mail** a message to the mailing list, and everybody on the mailing list gets your message.

Configuring Outlook Express for Use with Mailing Lists

You don't do anything special to configure Outlook Express for use with mailing lists. If you can send and receive e-mail with Outlook Express, you're ready to begin using Internet mailing lists.

Finding the Mailing List You Want

Many, many mailing lists exist. So it can be a little difficult to find one that matches your interest. The phrase "needle in a haystack" comes to mind. You can, however, get a list of mailing lists from this **anonymous FTP** site: *ftp://rtfm.mit.edu/pub/usenet/news.answers/mail/mailing-lists*. What you want to do is get the **file** named part01 and at least a few of the other "part" files listed at this site. To start, for example, get part02 and part03, print these text files (you can use the Windows WordPad utility to do this), and read through the stuff. Take it from there.

You can also find a good list of mailing lists at the web site *http://www.neosoft.com/internet/paml/*.

If either of the preceding uniform resource locators don't work, use a search service such as AltaVista to search on the terms "mailing list" or "publicly accessible mailing list."

Subscribing to a Mailing List Administered by a Person

To get your name added to a mailing list, you need to know the e-mail address of the mailing list administrator. You also need the specific instructions for subscribing to the mailing list. These differ for each list, but you can get them from one of the "lists of lists" described in the previous paragraph.

Here's an example. If I wanted to subscribe to the mailing list *Birdfeeder*, a mailing list about birdhouses and bird feeders, I would send the following e-mail message:

```
To:        birdfeeder-request@userhome.com
Message:   SUBSCRIBE
```

continues

Mailing List *(continued)*

A tip for new mailing list subscribers

You probably don't want to subscribe to a bunch of mailing lists right off the bat. Instead, subscribe to one. Or maybe two at the most. Otherwise, you'll find yourself overwhelmed with e-mail. And you don't want that to happen.

Unsubscribing from a Mailing List Administered by a Person

To have your name removed from a mailing list, you just e-mail a message to the list administrator's address. Usually, when you first subscribe to the mailing list, you receive a welcome letter that includes the instructions for unsubscribing to the list. It's a good idea to save this letter for future reference. Sometimes, each edition of the mailing list includes instructions for unsubscribing as well.

A mailing list faux pas

When you send a subscription request, be sure you send your e-mail message to the mailing list administrator. You don't want to send the subscription request to the mailing list. Oh no. If you do, you'll be mailing your request to everyone on the list. The mailing list administrator's e-mail address is usually named *list-request*, where *list* is the name of the mailing list. Does that make sense? So if the mailing list name is *birdfeeder*, the mailing list administrator's address is probably *birdfeeder-request*.

Subscribing to a Mailing List Administered by a Program

One point that is sort of confusing about this whole mailing list business is that some mailing lists aren't administered by a person. Some of them are administered by programs such as Majordomo, **LISTSERV**, or Listproc. If the **username** that you e-mail your subscription request to is, for example, Majordomo, LISTSERV, or Listproc, you are actually sending your subscription request to the program that administers the mailing list. To learn the correct name of the program, site, and domain, you probably have to get the skinny from someone who's already subscribed. Or you have to get more detailed information about the mailing list. (For example, you could get the mailing list subscription information from the **anonymous FTP** site I described earlier.)

Once you get this information, you subscribe by sending the administrator an e-mail message For example, to subscribe to the mailing list bagpipe, I would send my subscription request to *majordomo@piobaire.mines.uidaho.edu*. My e-mail message would look like this:

```
To:       majordomo@piobaire.mines.uidaho.edu
Message:  SUBSCRIBE BAGPIPE
```

Unsubscribing to a Mailing List Administered by a Program

To have your name removed from a mailing list administered by a program like Majordomo, LISTSERV, or Listproc, you just e-mail a message to the administrator and include the appropriate unsubscribe command. Which command you use to unsubscribe, however, depends on the mailing list administrator program.

For more help, request help

The mailing list administrator programs—Listproc, LISTSERV, and Majordomo—offer more commands than I've described here. You can usually get a list of the commands (with descriptions) that a mailing list administrator program uses by sending the one-word message "help" to the mailing list administrator.

SEE ALSO   E-Mail; FTP; Outlook Express

MAN

MAN has two meanings. The MAN acronym—all uppercase letters—stands for metropolitan area **network.** Not knowing this term wouldn't make you less of a person, but you do sometimes hear people use it. Especially technical types who want to distinguish this type of network from a **LAN,** or local area network, and a **WAN,** or wide area network.

The **UNIX** operating system provides a *man* command—all lowercase letters. The *man* command opens up a "manual" of online help. This nugget of knowledge is a good one to remember.

Megabyte

As you may already know, a byte is an eight-digit string of 1s and 0s that your computer uses to represent a character. This, for example, is the byte that represents the character A:

01010100.

A **kilobyte** is roughly 1000 of these bytes. (Or to be precise, a kilobyte is 1024 of these bytes.)

A megabyte is roughly 1,000,000 of these bytes. (Again, if you want to be precise, a megabyte is exactly 1,048,576 bytes. Oh my.)

Another way to look at a megabyte is in terms of how long it takes you to **download** or **upload** a megabyte of stuff. With your **modem** passing data through at a rate of 28,800bps, or 28.8Kbps, it would take around 5 minutes to download or upload one megabyte of data.

Microsoft Chat SEE Chat

Microsoft Exchange SEE Exchange

Microsoft FrontPage Express SEE FrontPage Express

Microsoft NetMeeting SEE NetMeeting

Microsoft NetShow Player SEE NetShow Player

Microsoft Network

Microsoft Network, or more precisely, The Microsoft Network, is the name of Microsoft's **online service.** I mention this here because The Microsoft Network provides an easy way to connect to the Internet. With the version of The Microsoft Network that's available as I'm writing this, you can browse the **World Wide Web** (including **FTP** sites), send and receive e-mail, participate in **mailing lists,** and read and post messages to **newsgroups.** To sign up for The Microsoft Network (or any other Internet service provider), you can use the **Connection Wizard** that comes with Internet Explorer.

Microsoft Outlook Express SEE Outlook Express

Microsoft Wallet SEE Wallet

MIME

MIME is an acronym for Multipurpose Internet Mail Extensions. MIME is a protocol that lets you attach binary files—like **JPEG** files, **GIF** files, **MPEG** files, and so on—to **e-mail** messages. As long as the people you send messages to also have e-mail readers that support the MIME protocol, they can extract and use the files you send them. For example, you could use MIME to attach a Microsoft Word for Windows document to an e-mail message. If the recipient's e-mail reader supports MIME, the recipient can extract the Word document from the e-mail message. If the recipient has a copy of Word for Windows, he or she can open and work with the document in Word.

While MIME is really useful, not all e-mail clients and not all e-mail servers support it. In this case, you can still send binary files in e-mail, but you need to use another tool called **uuencode.** You can also still receive binary files, but you will need to decode the attachments using a decoding utility.

Modem

A modem—the word means *modulator/demodulator*—is a hardware device for sending digital information like **files** and messages over telephone lines. To send this digital information, the modem converts computer data into sounds and sends the sounds over the telephone line to another modem and computer at the other end of the telephone line. To receive this digital information, the modem hears the sounds coming over the telephone line and converts the sounds back into digital code that a computer can read.

How fast a modem can send or receive data is measured in **bits per second,** or bps. Modems with higher bps rates can send and receive data faster. When you are shopping for a modem, buy a 14,400bps or 28,800bps model. They cost more, but you'll save money in the long run because you won't spend as much time using **online services,** which charge by the hour. Fast modems can download information quicker.

SEE ALSO   Baud; Downloading Files

Moderator

A moderator is someone who decides which **articles** are posted to a **newsgroup** or which e-mail messages are sent to the people on a **mailing list.** A newsgroup or mailing list that has one of these characters is called, cleverly enough, a moderated newsgroup or a moderated mailing list.

For the readers or users of a newsgroup or mailing list, moderators are wonderful. They make sure that people stay on track. And they weed out the silly articles and messages that waste people's time and disk space. In fact, if I were to offer a single suggestion for making the best use of your time with things like newsgroups and mailing lists, I'd suggest that you stick to those with moderators.

continues

Moderator *(continued)*

Unfortunately, if you're trying to post stuff to a newsgroup or send e-mail messages to a mailing list, moderators can be really frustrating. They might seem like censors. Sometimes they filter out the most cogent and poignant ideas. And, darn it, they always take a while to review the articles and messages you want to post. Almost as if they have a life outside their probably-unpaid duty as moderator. Perhaps they have jobs or families, for instance.

SEE ALSO   Netiquette

MPEG

MPEG is a graphics file format for video, or movies. (The acronym stands for Moving Pictures Experts Group.) Like **JPEG,** MPEG was developed to provide a very efficient and compressed format for storing high-quality video. To view an MPEG file, you need an MPEG viewer.

Multitasking

Multitasking refers to the running of more than one application at the same time. You may not think you care about this, but actually you do. Because Windows lets you smoothly multitask, you can be working away with your word processor, for example, at the same time as Internet Explorer is slaving away to download a huge file. Windows automatically multitasks Windows-based applications. Whenever you or Windows opens more than one Windows-based application, you're multitasking. Pretty cool, huh? To switch between the applications you're running, just click application buttons on the Taskbar.

SEE ALSO   Switching Tasks

My Computer

Internet Explorer lets you do more than just browse the World Wide Web. You can use Internet Explorer to also look at your local computer's disks, folders, and files. To use Internet Explorer in this way, start Internet Explorer and then choose the Go menu's My Computer command. When you do this, Internet Explorer displays the My Computer window.

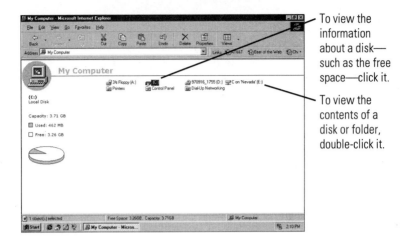

To view the information about a disk—such as the free space—click it.

To view the contents of a disk or folder, double-click it.

More about the Internet Explorer and the My Computer view

Almost everything you can do with **Windows Explorer** you can also do with My Computer. For example, you can open folders, programs, and documents; rename and delete folders and documents; and even access Control Panel tools.

Name Server SEE Domain Name Service

Netiquette

Netiquette is the special word that's been coined to describe Internet etiquette. You know what I'm describing here, right? Good manners. Proper conduct. That sort of thing. Fortunately, Internet etiquette—netiquette—isn't as complicated as the etiquette rules for going to dinner at, say, Buckingham Palace or the White House. There, so I've read, you have to know about all sorts of stuff. Like which of the four forks to use. (Actually, I happen to know the answer to this one: start with the fork farthest to the left and work your way inward, or toward the plate, as the courses arrive on the table. But back to the Internet...)

continues

Netiquette *(continued)*

On the Internet, you just have to be a nice guy or gal. If an organization lets you anonymously **telnet** or **FTP** to their host, follow any rules they suggest for usage. (Like hours the host can be accessed.) Don't flame people. Don't post articles that waste people's time to newsgroups (like a "Me, too!" message). Don't **spam**. Make sure you post articles to the correct newsgroup. And for gosh sakes, if you have a question about what is and is not proper netiquette, **lurk** or look for a **FAQ**.

SEE ALSO   RTFM; Shouting

NetMeeting

Microsoft NetMeeting is an Internet client that lets you communicate with other people over either the Internet or an **intranet.** Using NetMeeting, you can talk to other people, video-conference, share programs and documents, send and receive files, draw on a virtual whiteboard, and even **chat.** When you use NetMeeting to communicate with someone else, it's called an Internet Call.

Netscape Navigator

Netscape Navigator is another web browser. It competes with Microsoft's Internet Explorer. While you presumably use Internet Explorer as your web browser if you purchased or are reading this book, let me just say that most everything you read here about the Internet and web browsing applies with equal force to Netscape Navigator.

NetShow Player

Microsoft NetShow Player lets you play active streaming format, or ASF, files as well as live ASF streams. In a nutshell, what all this means is that Internet Explorer can use NetShow Player to play multimedia clips you've grabbed off of the Internet or an **intranet.**

Network

A network is just a bunch of computers that are connected together. Windows 95 and Windows 98, for example, let you create what are called peer-to-peer networks as long as you've got **Ethernet** cards installed in the computers and the right kind of cabling to connect the Ethernet cards. But I'm getting off the track. The reason I mention this is because the Internet is really a network of networks. But one thing I probably should mention is that while all of the individual networks, or subnets, that make up the Internet are **TCP/IP** networks, the individual hosts use a bunch of different operating systems. Some of these hosts use Windows for their operating system. But other hosts use **UNIX**, Windows NT, and even DEC and IBM mainframe and minicomputer operating systems.

Newbie

A newbie is someone who's new to the neighborhood—the Internet neighborhood, that is. Everybody on the Internet was a newbie once, of course. But many experienced veterans of the Internet forget this. So newbies often get picked on. In fairness to the oldtimers, newbies can become rather a nuisance on the Internet because many of them don't **lurk,** they ignore the **FAQs,** and they refuse to **RTFM.** Probably the best way to avoid this abuse is to be sensitive to the informal rules and protocols of the Internet, which will minimize mistakes on your part.

SEE ALSO   Netiquette

Newsgroup

A newsgroup is basically an electronic corkboard where people post and read messages related to a particular topic or interest. For free. And with more than 10,000 active newsgroups, there's a newsgroup on just about every topic imaginable. In fact, I think it's fair to say that newsgroups are probably one of the three most popular **resources** available on the Internet. (**E-mail** and the **World Wide Web** are the other two.)

To write messages for and read messages on a newsgroup, you need a newsgroup reader. Because this book is about Internet Explorer, I'm going to assume that you'll use **Outlook Express** (which comes with Internet Explorer) as your newsgroup reader.

continues

Newsgroup *(continued)*

Configuring Outlook Express as Your Newsgroup Reader

You shouldn't need to do anything special to use Outlook Express as your newsgroup reader. Technically, the only real prerequisite to using Outlook Express as a newsgroup reader is that you need to tell Outlook Express the name of your Internet service provider's news NNTP server. But you shouldn't have to worry about this specification. The **Connection Wizard** does this for you. If you have problems performing any of the actions described in the paragraphs that follow, call your Internet service provider and ask for help.

Checking Out and Subscribing to Newsgroups

In order to read and post to newsgroups, you need to first download the list of newsgroups available on your Internet service provider's news server and then you need to find newsgroups that interest you. To do this, follow these steps:

1 Start Outlook Express.

2 Choose the Go menu's News command.

3 Click the Newsgroups button. Outlook Express displays the Newsgroups dialog box.

4 Click the All tab to display a list of the newsgroups maintained by your Internet service provider's news server. (If this is the first time you've displayed the All tab of the Newsgroups dialog box, you may have to wait while Outlook Express retrieves a list of newsgroups from the Internet service provider's news server.)

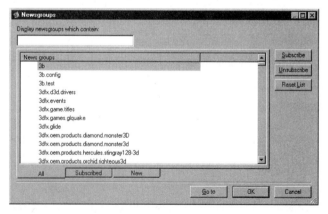

5 Enter a keyword in the text box to display all newsgroups that include that word, or alternately, scroll through the list of newsgroups until you find a newsgroup that you think might interest you.

6 Select the newsgroup, and then click the Go To button if you want to preview the newsgroup or click the Subscribe button to subscribe to the newsgroup. When you subscribe to a newsgroup, you add it to your list so that you can quickly access it, whereas if you preview the newsgroup, it disappears from your list as soon as you exit Outlook Express. (If you are working offline, you need to choose the Tools menu's Download This Newsgroup command to connect and download the article headers.)

Unsubscribing to Newsgroups

You can unsubscribe to newsgroups you no longer want to browse. To unsubscribe, display the Newsgroups dialog box as described in the preceding paragraphs. Then select the newsgroup, and click the Unsubscribe button.

Want to test out this posting business?

The busiest newsgroup you'll see is *alt.test*. It's the one you use to test whether your posting technique works. If you want to try out the steps I've described here, post to *alt.test*. To see if your message posted correctly, check that newsgroup in an hour or so. (Or check it tomorrow.) By the way, you'll get automatic **e-mail** responses from some of the **NNTP** sites that maintain the *alt.test* newsgroup. They send responses so you know your message got posted. If you don't want to see any of these responses, include the word "ignore" in your message header.

Reading Newsgroup Articles

After you have downloaded the article headers for a newsgroup, you can begin reading the individual articles. To do this, follow these steps:

1 Start Outlook Express.

2 Click the newsgroup you want to browse. Outlook Express retrieves a list of the articles posted to the newsgroup and displays this list in the right pane of the Outlook Express window.

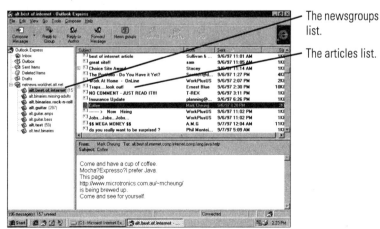

The newsgroups list.

The articles list.

continues

Newsgroup *(continued)*

3 When Outlook Express displays the articles in the newsgroup, click one you want to browse. Outlook Express opens the message and displays it in the message area of the Outlook Express window.

4 If you want to see an article in its own window, double-click the article and Outlook Express displays the article in its own message window. When you finish reading the message, close the message window by clicking its Close box.

Moving to another article

To read the previous article, press the Up arrow key. To read the next message, press the Down arrow key.

Saving Attachments

If a newsgroup article includes a binary file attachment, you can save the attachment. (The attachment will show in the article either as an icon or, in the case of a graphics image, as a picture of the image itself.) To save the attachment to your hard disk, follow these steps:

1 Right-click the icon or the image. Outlook Express displays a shortcut menu.

2 Choose the Save command. (The exact name of this command depends on the type of attachment.) Outlook Express displays the Save dialog box.

3 Name the file, and click OK.

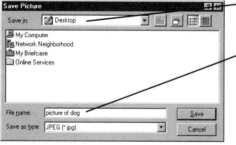

Optionally, use this box to specify where the file should be saved.

Use this box to name the attachment, or file.

Saving Attachments That Are Split Among Multiple Messages

Because some newsgroup readers and servers limit article sizes, people commonly break large attachments into several small pieces and then post individual pieces in separate messages. A 1MB attachment, for example, might be broken into five smaller pieces posted in five individual messages. (To identify these multipart attachments, people use message subject descriptions such as "File 1/5," "File 2/5," " File 3/5," and so on.) Outlook Express lets you easily download these message parts and combine the attachments. To download an attachment stored as several pieces across multiple messages, follow these steps:

1 Select the messages that hold the attachments. (You can do this by holding down the Ctrl key and then clicking each message.)

2 Right-click the selection.

3 Choose the Combine And Decode command. Outlook Express displays the Order For Decoding dialog box.

4 Verify that the messages appear in the right order—the first part first, the second part second, and so on. If the messages don't appear in the correct order, use the Move Up and Move Down buttons to arrange them correctly.

5 Click OK.

Posting Text-Only Articles

To post an article to a newsgroup, follow these steps:

1 Start Outlook Express.

2 Click the newsgroup to which you want to post an article.

3 Click the Compose Message button. Outlook Express displays the New Message window.

4 Create your article.

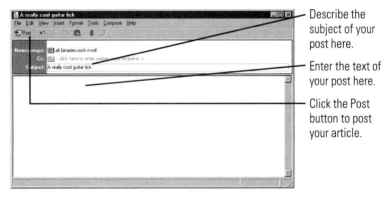

Describe the subject of your post here.

Enter the text of your post here.

Click the Post button to post your article.

5 To post the article, click the Post button. Outlook Express posts the article to the news server. (Note, however, that it may take a while for the news server to make the message available.)

Private replies

You can reply privately to the person who posted an article rather than to the newsgroup. To reply to an article privately, display the article in its own message window and then click the Reply To Author button. When Outlook Express displays the New Message window, enter your message and click Send.

Newsgroup (continued)

Posting Articles with Attachments

You post articles with attachments in almost the same manner as you post articles without attachments. To post an article with an attachment to a newsgroup, follow these steps:

1 Start Outlook Express.

2 Click the newsgroup to which you want to post an article.

3 Click the Compose Message button. Outlook Express displays the New Message window.

4 Create your article.

5 Click the Insert File button. Outlook Express displays the Insert Attachment dialog box.

6 Identify the attachment.

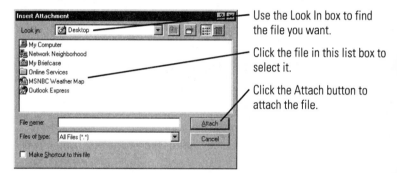

Use the Look In box to find the file you want.

Click the file in this list box to select it.

Click the Attach button to attach the file.

7 To post the article and its attachment, click the Post button. Outlook Express posts the article to the news server. (Again note, however, that it may take a while for the news server to make the message available.)

Some of you are curious, so I'll tell you

Okay, let's face up to a fact. One of the most notorious elements of the Internet is all the material on sexual themes. Presumably, you already know this, right? You've read the articles about people being arrested. You've read the articles about pornography being stored on university and government computer **networks.** I'm not telling you stuff you don't already know, right? You didn't just fall off the turnip truck. Since you already know all this stuff, you should know that for the most part the newsgroups are where all this stuff is stored. See the **Sex** entry if you want more information.

SEE ALSO   Free Speech; PGP

NNTP

This acronym stands for Network News Transfer Protocol. You sometimes see NNTP used as an adjective to describe a news **server**. Other than this, though, you won't really have to use this acronym. You don't, for example, use the acronym NNTP in **uniform resource locators**.

SEE ALSO   Newsgroup; Protocol

NSFnet

The NSFnet was a high-speed **network** of supercomputers connected by fiber-optic cables and microwave and satellite links. Until April of 1995, this network—it was funded by the National Science Foundation (NSF)—was the **backbone** of the Internet in the United States. What was the old NSFnet backbone is now controlled by SprintNet.

SEE ALSO   ARPA

Offline

Internet Explorer and Outlook Express let you work offline. What this means, basically, is that you can browse web pages, work with e-mail, and do a bit of work with newsgroups even when you're not connected to the Internet. When you work offline, of course, you can't retrieve web pages from the Internet. So you work with web pages you've stored in your **document cache** on your hard disk or in your history folder, or web pages to which you've subscribed.

If you want to work offline—by default Internet Explorer and Outlook Express assume you want to work online—choose the File menu's Work Offline command. (This command is available on the File menus of both Internet Explorer and Outlook Express.) If you try to retrieve a web page or some other item that hasn't been cached on your hard disk or you try to do something that requires a real connection, Internet Explorer or Outlook Express lets you know and asks if you want to make a connection.

SEE ALSO   Subscriptions

Online Services

The term *online services* refers to a big computer **network** with a
bunch of good **files** and programs. Whoever owns this big computer network makes money by selling people like you and me access to the files stored on the network and by renting us programs
on the network. Every online service, for example, provides **e-mail**
so you can e-mail other online service users. (Most online services—and perhaps all the online services—also provide e-mail
gateways to the Internet.) Online services also provide you with
other stuff. Usually, there are good games you can play, neat files
you can download, and up-to-the-minute news services that let you
know what's happening all over the world. The **Microsoft Network**
is an online service. So are **America Online**, CompuServe, and
Prodigy.

SEE ALSO   **Downloading Files; Outernet**

Outernet

A while back, someone coined the term *outernet* to point out a fact:
some **online services** aren't really part of the Internet even though
they are connected to the Internet via **gateways.** This doesn't mean
you should suddenly feel embarrassed or like less of a person because you're not really on the Internet. You're just on the outernet.
Because of the gateways, you can still do just about anything that
someone with a real Internet account can do. In addition, you get
whatever features the online service provides.

Outlook Express

Outlook Express is the e-mail **client** that comes with Internet Explorer, so this book assumes you'll use Outlook Express for **e-mail**
and for **mailing lists.** You also use Outlook Express for working
with **newsgroups.**

SEE ALSO   **Quick Reference: Outlook Express Commands *and* Outlook
Express Toolbar Guide**

Packets

Everything—all the information—that gets passed around the Internet is passed as a packet. When you send some piece of information, for example, it is broken down into packets by the sending computer and then reassembled by the receiving computer. In fact, this packetizing and unpacketizing is what the **TCP/IP** protocol does.

SEE ALSO   Gulf War; Packet-Switching Network

Packet-Switching Network

For all I know, you stumbled onto this entry by mistake. But since you're already here, let me explain why I included this entry in the book. The Internet, it turns out, is a packet-switching network. What this means is that when two computers communicate over the **network,** they break their data into **packets,** and then the packets get passed around the network. What's unique about a packet-switching network, at least when compared to a **circuit-switching network,** is that the packets don't have to travel on their own dedicated connection. In fact, one writer has used the analogy of the post office to explain what a packet-switching network is like. When you send something by **snail mail,** or regular mail, your letter or package doesn't get its own special airplane or mail truck. Instead, it gets bundled with a bunch of other people's mail. Only when the mail gets closer to its destination does it get separated into a little bundle of its own that the mail carrier drops into your mailbox.

A minor technical detail

There's another interesting aspect to a packet-switching network. Your packets don't have to travel the same route between the sending and receiving hosts. One packet might go through St. Louis on its way from Seattle to Miami. Another packet might instead go through Cincinnati even though this packet is part of the very same message.

SEE ALSO   Gulf War

continues

Password

You know what a password is, right? It's the secret word or code
that you give to a computer, along with your **username,** to prove
your identity. The logic of a password, of course, is that only the
real user knows the real password, so access to the computer can
be restricted to the person who is supposed to use it. There are,
however, three rules concerning passwords. One rule is that your
password shouldn't be easy to guess. (Don't use your name, for example.) The second rule is that you shouldn't forget your password.
The third rule is that you should never tell anyone your password.

PGP

PGP is an **encryption** utility. It encrypts—or turns into coded messages—electronic files such as **e-mail** messages. Once a message has
been encrypted using PGP, no one but the intended recipient can
read it. So PGP is sort of interesting to people who use the Internet.
Of more interest, however, is the story of how PGP was created and
what happened to the creator.

Briefly, in the mid-1980s, a college student named Phillip
Zimmerman read an article in the *Smithsonian* magazine that
described encryption algorithms (calculation rules, basically)
that made it nearly impossible for anyone other than the intended
recipient to read messages. So what did the kid do? Shoot, he did
what every good computer science student would do. Working
on his own, he created a software program that implements the
encryption algorithms.

Anyway, time goes by. By now it's the early 1990s and everything is
cruising along smoothly—until one day when one of Zimmerman's
friends posts Zimmerman's PGP utility on the Internet. The next
thing you know, people around the world are downloading copies
of this tool. And that was nice for them. But not for Zimmerman.

It turns out that the United States has strict export restrictions
that severely limit the ability of Americans and American companies from selling or distributing encryption technology. And
Zimmerman may have violated those export restrictions by making
PGP available on the Internet, because the Internet is a global network. In fact, for a while the U.S. Attorney's office in San Jose was

investigating Zimmerman's actions. He could have been imprisoned for as long as five years. And he could have been fined as much as $1 million. (At the time I'm writing this, things have apparently cooled off for Zimmerman.)

The story of PGP is a really good one, however, because it touches on a couple of important points about the Internet. First, the Internet is not a very secure network. Although not very likely, it's technically possible for text that gets passed around to be read by people if they want to read it. (This is why, so the rumor mill says, the U.S. doesn't want encryption technology distributed abroad: the Central Intelligence Agency and the National Security Agency want to electronically eavesdrop on people.)

A second thing that the PGP story shows is that it's easier than you think to break the law. Maybe Zimmerman or his friend knew that distributing the implementation of the algorithm—the same algorithm described in an internationally distributed magazine—would violate an export restriction. But I'll bet you a cup of coffee they didn't know. Part of the culture of the Internet is that you give back, that you post valuable information or utilities for the benefit of other people. Yet by posting PGP, Zimmerman got into serious trouble.

And there are lots of other similar cases—situations in which an Internet user got into trouble by posting stuff. Right now, for example, two Californians are serving jail time for posting explicit pictures to adult **newsgroups.** Their pictures violated pornography laws in Tennessee, even though they posted the stuff in California and even though their material may not have violated pornography laws in California. And more than a few people have gotten into trouble by posting e-mail messages and newsgroup **articles** that made libelous statements about other people or companies.

So another lesson of the PGP story is that before you post anything anywhere, think carefully. You don't want to post something that violates a federal law or some obscure federal regulation. And you need to be careful, too, that you don't unwittingly break a local law in some other part of the country.

continues

PGP *(continued)*

In a nutshell, how PGP works

How PGP works is sort of interesting. The whole encryption system relies on two keys, a public key and a private key. What you do (if you have PGP) is freely distribute the public key. Anyone who has PGP and your public key can use the public key to lock messages they send to you. Whenever you get a PGP-encrypted message, you unlock the message with the private key. The whole system works because, while anyone with the public key can lock a message, only the person with the correct private key can unlock it.

SEE ALSO   Digital ID

Pine

Pine is a popular **e-mail** software program developed, coincidentally, by my alma mater, the University of Washington. If you're connecting to the Internet using a **shell account** and the **HyperTerminal** application, for example, there's a good chance you're using pine. Because this book assumes that you're connecting to the Internet using Internet Explorer (which means you aren't using a shell account), I'm not going to provide any step-by-step instructions here.

Ping

Remember that game the neighbor kids played when you were a kid? The one where you run up to someone's door, ring the bell, and then run away? Well, that's sort of what ping does. In effect, ping rings the doorbell of an Internet **host** to see if the Internet host will answer. Then it runs away. With ping, however, this doorbell-ringing business isn't just for fun. By pinging a host, you can tell whether it will respond. In fact, if you're trying to connect to a host but can't, you can try pinging the host. If you can't successfully ping the host, it probably means that the host is either shut down or is not responding to anything, or that a part of the Internet between you and this other host is shut down.

Using Ping

To use ping, follow these steps:

1 Start MS-DOS. One way to do this is to click Start and then choose Programs and MS-DOS Prompt.

2 Change to the Windows directory, since this is where the ping client is probably stored.

3 Type ping at the MS-DOS prompt followed by the IP address of the host you want to ping.

More on ping

If you type the ping command but don't include an IP address, ping lists a bunch of command parameters you can enter after the IP address to control the way ping pings.

The loopback address

There's a loopback IP address, 127.0.0.1, that you should always be able to ping. That's because, for the purposes of ping, your computer's IP address is 127.0.0.1. I mention this only because you'll sometimes see a nasty little joke in play on the Internet. Some **newbie** can't seem to connect. So somebody tells the newbie to ping the IP address 127.0.0.1 "just to see if you're really connected to the Internet." The newbie can of course ping 127.0.0.1, since that's his or her machine. And by this time the newbie is totally confused. "Gee," the newbie thinks, "Ping says I'm connected, but I can't seem to do anything...." And so it goes, with everyone getting a good laugh at the newbie's expense.

Pirates

If you've read much of this book or you've surfed the Internet, you're not going to be surprised by what I say next: there's a dark side to the Internet. No, it's not that the technology is dehumanizing. Or that the Internet is a stepping stone on the path to some Orwellian future. The dark side stems from the "pirates." "Who are the pirates?" you ask. (Pirates are also known by another name, "crackers.") Good question. These are the guys who break into **host** computers and then steal the information stored there or store their own information there. This maybe sounds innocuous, but it's really not. What they're sometimes stealing are things like people's credit card numbers. And what they're often storing are pornography or stolen software. I'm not sure that there's anything you (or I) can do about all this. But I think you should be aware that while most of the people you run into on the Internet are wonderful, there are a handful of dirtballs.

PKUNZIP SEE PKZIP

PKZIP

PKZIP is a popular compression utility that scrunches **files** so they take less space. How compression utilities scrunch files is beyond the scope of our little discussion. But if you frequently e-mail large attachments to people, you'll want to acquire and then regularly use a compression utility such as PKZIP. The reason is that scrunching a file makes it easier to move the file around the Internet. That makes sense, right? A file that is 100KB in size, all other factors being equal, will take longer to **download** and **upload** than a file that is 20KB in size.

You should be able to find an evaluation of PKZIP or WinZip, which is an equivalent compression utility at the following web site: *http://www.zdnet.com/*.

The dirt on compression

The amount of compression you get with PKZIP (and any other file compression utility, for that matter) varies wildly because it depends on the type of file you're compressing. Sometimes PKZIP doesn't reduce the size of a file very much at all. If you try to PKZIP a GIF file, for example, you'll often get no real compression. The same is true of a **JPEG** file. Other graphics file formats, however, scrunch to 1 or 2 percent of their original size. While compression can sometimes make files much, much smaller—and it's probably something you should try—it doesn't always deliver a benefit.

SEE ALSO   Downloading Files

Plug-In

Web browsers like Internet Explorer use special programs, called plug-ins, to do work they're not capable of doing themselves. For example, Internet Explorer can't show audio clips, so to play these sorts of sounds, it uses an audio plug-in. Internet Explorer also can't run video clips, so to play videos, it uses a video plug-in. Web page animation typically requires a plug-in, too.

Port

Sometimes you need to specify a port number as part of the **uniform resource locator** (URL). The port doesn't have anything to do with the serial or parallel ports your computer uses to connect to devices like **modems** and printers. Rather, a port specifies which connection your session uses to connect to the **server.** I should say that you probably won't ever have to worry about this port business. But if you see a URL that looks like the one that follows, the number that gets tagged onto the end of everything else is the port number:

```
telnet://locis.loc.gov:3000
```

The port number is 3000. I just made up this URL, by the way. So don't try to telnet there.

PPP

PPP stands for Point-to-Point Protocol. It describes a method of connecting to the Internet in which your PC, for the duration of the connection, becomes a **host** computer on the Internet. The advantage of a PPP connection is that it simplifies the business of **downloading** and **uploading files,** as compared to just having a **shell account.** With a PPP connection, you can move **files** directly between another host and your PC. (If you use a shell account, you first move a file from some other host to your Internet service provider's computer and then from your Internet service provider's computer to your PC.) A PPP connection also lets you use a web **browser** like the **Internet Explorer** to browse the **World Wide Web.** The only disadvantages of a PPP connection are that Internet service providers usually charge more money for them and they are slightly more difficult to set up. (You either use the **Connection Wizard** or **Dial-Up Networking** to make a PPP connection.)

SEE ALSO   Downloading Files; SLIP

Protocol

In the world of diplomacy, a "protocol" refers to the rules of etiquette and ceremony that diplomats and heads of state follow. For example, "Don't drink from your finger bowl" is a protocol.

In the world of computers, "protocol" refers to the rules that two computers use to communicate. For example, "Don't send me data faster than I can receive it" is a very basic computer protocol.

SEE ALSO   HyperTerminal; IP; TCP/IP; Zmodem

RealPlayer

RealPlayer is a **plug-in** that lets you play RealAudio audio and RealVideo video clips you retrieve from the Internet. Typically, you play RealAudio and RealVideo clips by clicking a **hyperlink** that points to the clip. When you click the hyperlink, Internet Explorer starts the RealPlayer plug-in.

Remote Access Service

Remote Access Service, another name for Dial-Up Networking, is the Windows feature that lets you connect your personal computer to the Internet. As a practical matter, you don't ever have much to do with Remote Access Service, or Dial-Up Networking, because the **Connection Wizard** sets up all the Remote Access Service stuff for you.

Resource

When I first started reading about the Internet, I kept stumbling across the term *resource*. I found it really confusing. It finally dawned on me that people used the term to refer to a bunch of different things that were all sort of alike.

People sometimes use the term as a catchall category to refer to an Internet service such as a **newsgroup,** the **World Wide Web,** or **FTP.** Other times, the word refers to specific **servers**—mail servers, news servers, World Wide Web servers, Gopher servers, FTP servers, and so on. Still other times it refers to specific **files** (and their locations).

I think the most accurate way to use the term is to refer to something that can be described with a **uniform resource locator.** That's the way I use the term in this book. I use it to refer both to servers and to specific files. This is probably all crystal clear to you now. And you're wondering why I had trouble in the first place.

ROT13

ROT13 is a code. People sometimes use it to encrypt newsgroup articles that they don't want other people to read by mistake. For example, if you posted an article with information or commentary that was offensive to some people, you could encrypt the article using the ROT13 code. By doing this, you'd be in effect warning people, "Hey, there's some pretty strong stuff in this message. You probably don't want to read it if you're easily offended."

continues

ROT13 *(continued)*

The ROT13 code is easy to break, however. Anyone who really wants to can break the code and read a message that has been encrypted with the ROT13 code. In fact, Outlook Express's Edit menu includes a command, Unscramble (ROT13), that you can use to decrypt the newsgroup article shown in the message window. (This command only appears on the Edit menu when you've opened a newsgroup article in a message window.)

SEE ALSO   Digital ID; Encryption; Newsgroup

RTFM

You see this acronym in postings to **newbies** a lot. But I wouldn't suggest using it unless you know what the letter "F" stands for. The R, T, and M stand for "Read The Manual."

Scripting

Some communications applications provide a scripting feature. In a nutshell, a scripting feature types stuff for you. Your **username,** your **password,** and anything else you're supposed to type as you make a connection. While the **HyperTerminal** application doesn't provide such a feature, the **Dial-Up Networking** application (which you use to make **PPP** connections) does. To write a Dial-Up Networking script—let's say you aren't using the **Connection Wizard** but are instead doing things manually—you use the Dial-Up Scripting Tool.

Search Engine

Search engines are services that help you find what you're looking for on the Internet. These services are so valuable that most web browsers have a search tool or command that you can click to display a list of search engines.

Using a Search Engine

To use a search engine, you display the search engine's form (which is just a web page with buttons and boxes), usually by clicking a button. When your web browser displays the search engine form, you enter the word or phrase you want the search engine to use in its search. (To narrow your search, be very specific.) When you click the search engine form's Start Search button (this might be named Start, Submit, Go, or some similar name), the search engine looks through its index for web pages that use the word or phrase you entered. If the search engine finds web pages that use your word or phrase, it displays a results web page, which describes and provides hyperlinks to the web pages.

One other comment. Each search engine works a little differently, so you'll have to experiment to find which one best suits your needs. You'll also want to learn to use one search service really well. (You can do this by reading all the instructions provided by the search engine.)

Locating a Search Service

The following table lists some of the largest and most comprehensive search indexes, but keep in mind that there are thousands (and perhaps even millions) of smaller search engines that index only those web sites relating to specialized fields or from certain geographic regions.

Search engine	Uniform resource locator
AltaVista	http://www.altavista.digital.com
Excite	http://www.excite.com
Infoseek	http://www.infoseek.com
Lycos	http://www.lycos.com
WebCrawler	http://www.webcrawler.com
Yahoo!	http://www.yahoo.com

Server

When you use your PC to connect directly to another **host computer**—for example, when you use a **Dial-Up Networking** connection—your PC is called a **client**. The other host computer is a **server**. Since we're on the topic, I may as well also say that the software that runs on the client is client software. And the software that runs on the server is—big surprise here—server software.

One point that's good to remember is that to do just about anything, your client software and the server software need to work together. Oftentimes you can't accomplish some task, even though the client and its software work, because either the server or its software doesn't work.

Sex

There's a ton of sexually oriented material in Internet **newsgroups** such as *alt.sex.stories* and *alt.binaries.pictures.erotica*. There are also a handful of **World Wide Web** sites that offer sexual material, including *http://www.playboy.com* and *http://www.penthousemag.com*. Some of this stuff is tame, and some is very explicit. Some of this stuff qualifies as art. And some of it is disgusting. I think the disgusting stuff mostly appears in newsgroups without **moderators.** But I'm not sure. I have not done exhaustive research on this.

SEE ALSO   Free Speech

Shareware

Shareware is software that is given away free. If you like the software or intend to use it, you are supposed to send a small fee to the programmer who created it. Some shareware applications have code written into them that makes the programs inoperable unless users pay the fee within a certain period of time. Besides computer applications, clip art collections and font files are distributed as shareware. In fact, I think it's fair to say that the Internet's **FTP** sites and **newsgroups** are chock-full of shareware.

Freeware, a variation of shareware, is given away absolutely free. You don't have to send any money to the programmer who invented it, although most programmers ask for a postcard or some other gratis acknowledgment. I guess they want to know who's using their software.

Shell Account

With a shell account, you use a communications application like **HyperTerminal** to connect to an **Internet service provider.** Your PC becomes, in effect, just a monitor and keyboard attached to the Internet service provider's **host computer.** Although shell accounts were once commonplace among Internet users, most people now use Dial-Up Networking accounts because they are easier to use and they allow users to graphically browse the World Wide Web.

SEE ALSO   Connections

Shortcut Icons

Windows lets you place icons for commonly used documents, web pages, programs, **folders,** and other stuff like this on the **desktop.** This maybe doesn't seem like all that neat of a deal, but it is. By putting one of these icons, called shortcut icons, on the desktop, you can open a program such as Internet Explorer or some other Internet client with a simple double-click. (The **Internet** setup program adds a shortcut icon for the **Internet Explorer** to the desktop. But you may want to add shortcut icons for other client software programs, such as **FTP** and **telnet.**)

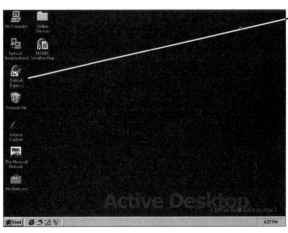

This is a shortcut icon. Windows uses an icon that identifies the application it will instruct to open the program—in this case, the Outlook Express **client.**

continues

Shortcut Icons *(continued)*

Creating a Shortcut Icon

To create a shortcut icon for an Internet **client** such as FTP or telnet, follow these steps:

1 Start Windows Explorer.

2 Select the client, or program, for which you want to create the shortcut icon. (You may need to select the folder that holds the client first.)

3 Choose the File menu's Create Shortcut command. Windows Explorer adds a shortcut to the folder.

4 Drag the shortcut to the desktop. Windows Explorer moves the shortcut icon to the desktop.

Shouting

If you type an **e-mail** message or a **newsgroup** article in all capital letters, it's called shouting. BUT YOU SHOULDN'T DO THIS. IT'S ANNOYING AS ALL GET OUT. What's more, type in all capital letters is hard to read.

SEE ALSO   Netiquette

Signature

A signature is just an extra little bit of text you attach to the end of every **e-mail** message you send. If you use **Outlook Express** as your e-mail program, you can add signatures to your e-mail messages. To do this, follow these steps:

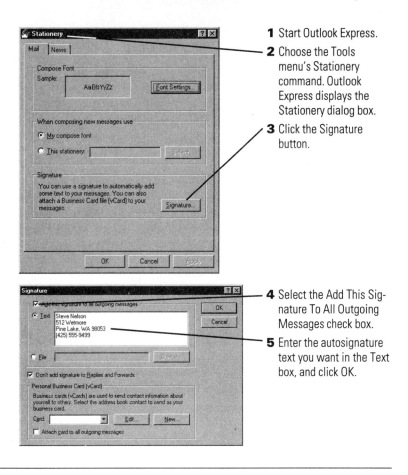

1 Start Outlook Express.

2 Choose the Tools menu's Stationery command. Outlook Express displays the Stationery dialog box.

3 Click the Signature button.

4 Select the Add This Signature To All Outgoing Messages check box.

5 Enter the autosignature text you want in the Text box, and click OK.

SLIP

SLIP is an acronym for Serial Line Internet Protocol. Like **PPP,** it is a method of directly connecting to the Internet. When you make a SLIP connection, your PC becomes a **host computer** on the Internet for the duration of the connection. The advantage of a SLIP connection (and a PPP connection) is that it simplifies the business of **downloading** and **uploading files,** as compared to a **shell account** connection. With a SLIP or PPP connection, you move a file only once (from the host that acts as the **server** to your PC) rather than twice (first from the host that acts as the server to the **Internet service provider's** computer and then from the Internet service provider's computer to your PC).

continues

SLIP *(continued)*

A SLIP connection also lets you do things like browse the **World Wide Web.** The only two disadvantages of a SLIP connection are that Internet service providers usually charge more money for them and they are slightly more difficult to set up. (You use the **Dial-Up Networking** program to make a SLIP connection.)

SLIP vs. PPP

If you have a choice between a PPP or SLIP connection, choose PPP. PPP is pretty much the standard these days. Plus, PPP is faster than SLIP. What's more, it's easier to set up a PPP connection. No matter how you got Windows on your machine, you have all the stuff you need already. (The SLIP stuff comes only on the CD version of Windows.) Finally, some of the stuff you have to do to set up a SLIP connection is rather complicated. You have to worry about **IP** header compression, for example. Yuck.

Smileys

E-mail, like any writing, isn't a very precise communication tool. It's easy to say too much. Or too little. Or to leave the reader confused or angry. And this is true even if you're the world's greatest living novelist (or so I imagine). To deal with the limitations of the written word in e-mail, people sometimes add smileys, also called emoticons, to their messages. In essence, a smiley is a face you make with symbol keys. For example, by combining the colon with the end parenthesis mark—turn the page sideways to see this—you get a smiley face. Sort of.

:)

And if you combine the colon with the begin parenthesis mark, you get a frowning face:

: (

Lots of people—and you may be one—find it helpful to use these faces to say what their prose doesn't say. Do smileys work? I don't know. You be the judge:

Sue,

I'm sorry I missed you.

I thought we had a date. But I guess not.

See you around the playground.

Steve

: (

Snail Mail

Snail mail is what Internet users sometimes call the regular mail. You know, the kind with letters, envelopes, stamps, and letter carriers. Whereas it may take days, weeks, or even months for an airmail letter to reach some parts of the world, an e-mail message can move around the world in a matter of seconds. (I should probably tell you, however, that **e-mail** isn't always this fast, nor is it 100 percent reliable. Sometimes an e-mail message can take hours, days, or even weeks to reach its destination if the mail **servers** that do the work of delivering the message are slow or shut down.)

Spam

Spam refers to junk **e-mail.** Although spam may sound innocuous at first blush, it actually represents a big problem. Let me explain. What happens with spam is that somebody who wants to sell something—lets say it's investment advice—builds a list of thousands and thousands of **e-mail addresses.** (Special spam mailing programs can do this by looking at the e-mail names and addresses of the people who post messages to **newsgroups** and by looking at online directories of e-mail names and addresses.) Once the spammer has this list, he begins sending huge volleys of junk e-mail messages to the names on his mailing list. He may also sell his mailing list to other spammers. Suddenly you have thousands and thousands of spammers all sending thousands and thousands of junk e-mail messages. This affects you personally in at least two ways: First, you may rather quickly find your inbox littered with junk e-mail messages (which causes all the same problems that junk **snail mail** does). Second, the high volume of spam that's being passed around the Internet—on some mail **servers** spam accounts for 80 to 90 percent of the message volume—means that spam wastes **bandwidth.**

SEE ALSO Flame; Netiquette

Start Page

A start page is the first **World Wide Web** document you view with a web **browser** such as **Internet Explorer.** (Sometimes people also call start pages by another name, **home pages.**) You can tell your web browser which start page, or home page, it should display when you first start it. Or you can just use whatever start page the web browser is initially set to use.

Changing Your Start Page

You can specify which web page you want Internet Explorer to display when you start the program and when you click the Home button. The easiest way to do this is to first display the web page you want to use as your start page. Next, choose the View menu's Internet Options command. In the Internet Options dialog box, click the General tab and then click the Use Current button.

Returning to Your Start Page

To return to your start page, click the Home button, which appears on the Internet Explorer toolbar.

Stationery

Outlook Express, the e-mail client that comes with Internet Explorer, lets you use nicely formatted, professionally designed templates as the basis of the e-mail messages you create. With these templates—Outlook Express calls them stationery—you don't have to do any special formatting to your message. All you do is add the text.

To create a new e-mail message that uses stationery, start Outlook Express and then choose the Compose menu's New Message Using command. Outlook Express displays a submenu that lists the stationery choices you have. Select the command that corresponds to the stationery you want to use. Then compose your e-mail message in the usual way.

This message uses the Running Birthday stationery.

SEE ALSO   E-Mail

Subfolder

This book uses the term *subfolder* to refer to a **folder** within a folder. Some people might also call a subfolder a subdirectory.

Subscriptions

Internet Explorer lets you list web pages that you want to regularly view in a subscriptions list. Once you "subscribe"—all this means is that you've added the web page to your list—Internet Explorer will automatically check the web page to see if it's changed since the last time you viewed it and, optionally, will download the web page so you can view it.

Subscribing to a Web Page

To subscribe to a web page, follow these steps:

1 Display the web page.

2 Choose the Favorites menu's Add To Favorites command. Internet Explorer displays the Add Favorite dialog box.

3 Click the option button that corresponds to your subscription choice.

continues

Subscriptions *(continued)*

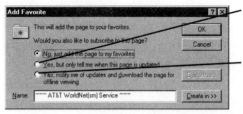

Click this option button if you want to be alerted of changes to the web page.

Click this option button if you want to download new copies of the web page for offline viewing.

Managing Your Subscriptions List

To see a list of your subscriptions, start Internet Explorer and then choose the Favorites menu's Manage Subscriptions command.

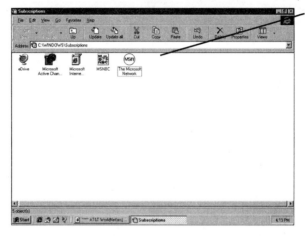

This is a subscriptions list.

To delete a subscription, click it and then click the Delete button.

To update a subscription, click it and then click the Update button. (You can also click the Update All button to update all your subscriptions.)

Scheduling Automatic Subscription Updates

To schedule an automatic subscription update, follow these steps:

1 Choose the Favorites menu's Manage Subscriptions command.

2 Right-click the subscription you want to automatically update. Choose the shortcut menu's Properties command. Internet Explorer displays the subscription's Properties dialog box.

3 Click the Schedule tab.

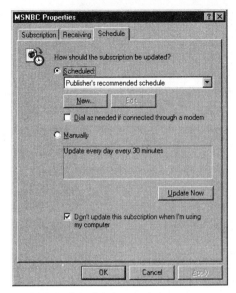

4 Click the Scheduled option button.

5 Select an update frequency from the Scheduled drop-down list box.

6 If you connect to the Internet using a Dial-Up Networking connection and a modem, select the Dial As Needed check box to tell Internet Explorer to automatically make an Internet connection to update your subscription.

7 If you don't want Internet Explorer to update a subscription while you're using your computer, select the Don't Update check box.

Getting notification about subscription updates

By default, Internet Explorer alerts you when subscription updates occur so that you can view updated web pages offline. You can change the way you receive this notification, however, by displaying the subscription's Properties dialog box, clicking the Receiving tab, and then using its buttons and boxes to specify how a subscription works.

SEE ALSO   Offline

Switching Tasks

To switch tasks in Windows, use the Taskbar. The Taskbar is the bar along the bottom of the screen. (If Internet Explorer is set to fullscreen, click the Fullscreen button to display the Taskbar.) The Taskbar shows the Start button on the left side. To the right of the Start button are buttons that represent applications that are open.

To open a new program, use the Start button. With Windows, you can run several applications at the same time.

To switch to an application that is open, click its button.

SEE ALSO   Multitasking

T1 Transmission Line

A T1 transmission line connects **host computers** and passes information at a rate of 1.5Mbps. That's pretty fast. Sometimes abbreviations like Mbps confuse people. So let's look at all of this in a table without the acronyms.

The lingo	Transmission speed
2400bps modem	2,400 bits (1s or 0s) per second
14.4K modem	14,400 bits per second
1.5Mbps T1 line	1,500,000 bits per second
45Mbps T3 line	45,000,000 bits per second

When I first heard about T1 transmission lines, I thought I needed one. Partly for the **bandwidth,** but also because my brother has one (he does research at a university). Alas, I soon learned that T1 lines are very, very expensive. Even if you have a short connection to make to another nearby host computer, you'll pay at least several hundred dollars a month—and very possibly a couple of thousand dollars a month. If you have a long connection to make to a faraway host computer, you could pay thousands of dollars a month. So I don't have a T1 transmission line.

High bandwidth doesn't always equal high performance

Many otherwise sophisticated people share a common misconception concerning those high-bandwidth transmission lines I just mentioned. Because the Internet is a **packet-switching network,** if you have a T1 transmission line, you quite likely share your transmission line with a bunch of other people. And because you share it, it may be that rather than personally moving 1.5Mbps on a T1 transmission line, you and nine of your fellow users simultaneously move data at a perceived rate of roughly 150Kbps. Or maybe you and 99 of your fellow users simultaneously move data at a perceived rate of roughly 15Kbps. Collectively, you guys are moving 1.5Mbps. But no one user gets all the bandwidth. This whole confusion, by the way, stems from the fact that people think the Internet works like a **circuit-switching network,** which it doesn't.

SEE ALSO Baud; Cable Modem

T3 Transmission Line

A T3 transmission line moves data at a rate of 45Mbps. That's really fast. In fact, the old **NSFnet** backbone used T3 transmission lines. And **online services** such as The **Microsoft Network** use T3 transmission lines as well.

SEE ALSO T1 Transmission Line

TCP/IP

TCP/IP is the **protocol** that describes how information gets passed around the Internet. (A protocol is essentially a set of rules.) TCP/IP breaks information into **packets,** routes those packets from the sending computer to the receiving computer, and finally reassembles the packets once they reach the receiving computer. If a packet is missing—say it gets lost somewhere on its trip from the sending computer—TCP/IP directs the sending computer to send another copy of the missing packet.

TCP/IP stands for Transmission Control Protocol/Internet Protocol, if you care to know, and I wouldn't blame you if you didn't.

SEE ALSO   Gulf War

Telnet

When you telnet, you **log on** to another computer or **network.** Okay. This sounds kooky, I know. But say you're logged on to an **Internet service provider's** computer or network. And you've been noodling around. Using a telnet command, you can probably log on to another computer network. In other words, even if you are 5000 miles away from the computer or network you want to log on to, you can use the Internet to make the connection.

Windows comes with a telnet client. To use it, you can enter the **uniform resource locator** (URL) for a telnet site in the Internet Explorer Address box, you can click on a **hyperlink** that points to a telnet site, or you can start the telnet client directly using **Windows Explorer.**

Starting a Telnet Session with Internet Explorer

As mentioned in the preceding paragraph, you can start a Telnet session with Internet Explorer in two ways: you can enter the URL for the telnet site in the Address box, and you can click on a hyperlink that points to a telnet site.

To enter the URL for a telnet site in the Address box, click the Address box to select its contents and then type the URL. Note that telnet sites start with the prefix "telnet://". When you press the Enter key, Internet Explorer starts the telnet client and instructs it to connect to the telnet site you identified.

To connect to a telnet site by clicking a hyperlink, you just click the hyperlink. (The hyperlink provides the telnet site's URL.) Internet Explorer starts the telnet client, and it connects to the telnet site identified with the hyperlink.

Once you connect to the telnet site, you follow the on-screen instructions provided by the telnet site.

Starting a Telnet Session with the Telnet Client

To start a Telnet session without Internet Explorer, first start the telnet client. (The telnet client probably is located in the Windows **folder.**) Then to make your telnet connection, follow these steps:

1 Choose the Connect menu's Remote System command. (If you haven't yet connected to your Internet service provider, this is when Windows makes the PPP connection.)

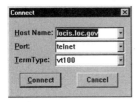

2 Enter the **host name** for the telnet site in the Host Name drop-down list box.

3 If necessary, enter the telnet **port** number in the Port drop-down list box.

4 If necessary, specify a terminal emulation type by using the Term Type drop-down list box.

5 Click Connect. Telnet makes the connection. Next you see either the logon screen for the telnet site (it asks for a username or user ID and a password) or you see the main menu if there isn't a formal logon.

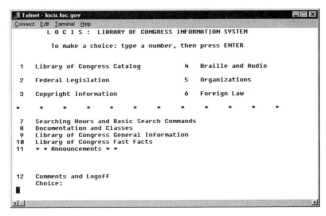

continues

Telnet *(continued)*

Ending a Telnet Session

To end a Telnet session, choose the Connect menu's Disconnect command. To stop the Telnet program and close the Telnet window, click the Telnet window's Close box.

SEE ALSO Port; Troubleshooting: Telnet; Quick Reference: Telnet Commands

Temporary Internet Files SEE Document Cache

Thread

As you might know, the messages that people post to **newsgroups** are called **articles**. You might also know that people can post articles that respond to other articles. The original article that someone posts along with any responses that other people post is called a thread.

TIN

TIN is a newsgroup reader that many Internet service providers give to people with **shell accounts**. You don't need to know how to work with TIN because you can use Internet Explorer. However, you might run into the term if you frequent **newsgroups**.

Uniform Resource Locator

The uniform resource locator, or URL, specifies how you find an Internet **resource**. There are four parts to a uniform resource locator: the service or **protocol**; the **server** name; the path; and the document, or file, name.

A Sample URL Explained

Let me explain each part of a URL by using a real-life Web page—the one that provides biographical data on the President of the United States and his family.

`http://www.whitehouse.gov/WH/glimpse/presidentshtml/bc42.html.`

http:// identifies this resource as part of the **World Wide Web.**

www.whitehouse.gov/ identifies the server. (Notice that whitehouse.gov is really a **domain name.**)

WH/glimpse/presidents/html/ names the directory and subdirectory within the World Wide Web document.

bc42.html names the World Wide Web document.

Reviewing the Other Services and Protocols

The World Wide Web is only one of the services available on the Internet. Not surprisingly then, URLs use other codes to identify the other services and protocols. Here's a list of codes with some examples and additional comments:

Service *or* protocol	Explanation
file://	Refers to a file on the local computer.
ftp://	Refers to the file transfer protocol.
gopher://	Refers to the **Gopher** service.
http://	Refers to the HyperText Transfer Protocol (**HTTP**), which is what you use to browse the World Wide Web.
news://	Refers to the network news transfer protocol, which is what you use to browse **newsgroups.**
telnet://	Used to start a **Telnet** session.

The URL blues

You can make a couple of easy mistakes when it comes to URLs. One is to mistakenly use backward slashes (\) instead of forward slashes (/). For example, the correct URL is *http://www.microsoft.com/*, not *http:\\www.microsoft.com*. The other easy mistake concerns case. **UNIX** operating systems recognize case (lower vs. upper) in filenames although not in server names. So if the URL is *http://www.blah.com/file.html* and you enter *http://www.blah.com/FILE.HTML*, it probably won't work. Note, however, that the URLs *http://www.blah.com/file.html* and *http://WWW.BLAH.COM/file.html* are equivalent. In other words, case doesn't matter for the server name. Let me say one last thing. You'll usually be fine if you use all lowercase letters.

SEE ALSO HTML

UNIX

If you're going to surf the Internet, you may come into frequent contact with UNIX because many Internet **hosts** use UNIX. (This might happen, for example, if you **telnet** to a UNIX host.) So I'm going to give you quick descriptions of a handful of common UNIX commands.

Note, however, that *many* different "flavors" of UNIX systems are used out there. I've tried to stick with the most common commands, but if you run into trouble, you may need to use the UNIX *man* command ("man" stands for "manual") to make sure some of the less common commands work on the machine you are connected to. (The *man* command is also a good way to see some of the additional commands and flags that are available.)

Command	Description
^C *or* ^X Ctrl+C *or* Ctrl+X)	These commands stop UNIX while it is performing a command. If I accidentally asked UNIX to list all the directories and subdirectories on the host computer, it could take hours, so I might use these commands to interrupt the computer and tell it to stop. (Note: Because computers are so fast at processing these commands, it could take a while for the output on the monitor to catch up to the work the computer has done. It will look as though the commands haven't affected anything, even though the computer has already stopped. Be patient.)
apropos *word*	Looks through the manual and gives you every instance of the word you ask for. Use it if you're not sure what you're looking for.
cd *directoryname*	Changes the working directory to the specified directory.
ls *filename* or *directoryname*	Displays a **filename** or the contents of a directory, *except* any files beginning with a period ("dot"). These are special configuration files, such as .SIGNATURE, .CSHRC, .LOGOUT, etc. If you don't specify a filename or directory name, the command shows the contents of the current directory.
ls -a	Lists all the files in the current directory, *including* those that begin with a dot.
ls -C *directoryname*	Lists all the files in a multicolumn format, instead of one name to a line. The number of columns is set automatically by the system. (You can change the number of columns, but doing so is very complicated.)

Command	Description
ls -F	Displays a slash (/) after the name if it's a directory and an asterisk (*) after the name if it can be executed (like a program). A few other signs are used for other types of files.
ls -R	Displays the names of any files, directories, subdirectories, sub-subdirectories, and so on, related to the work directory.
man *command*	Lists the help information for the command. ("Man" stands for "manual," so you can think of this as the host computer "help file.")
rm *filename*	Deletes the file from the UNIX host. The wildcards that are used for the MS-DOS DEL command may also be used here.
rm -i *filespecification*	When trying to delete more than one file, the -i flag tells the computer to ask whether you really want to delete the file before it deletes it. This is a great precaution to take, particularly if you're not comfortable with UNIX yet.
rm -r *directoryname*	Removes directories and their contents, including all subdirectories. In the beginning, it might be wise to combine this flag with the -i flag so that you are prompted at every stage of file and directory deletion.
rz *filename*	Used when you want the host computer to receive a file you are sending from your computer.
rz -b *filename*	Receives the file from you in binary format.
rz -p *filename*	Receives the file only if there is no file by that name in the receiving directory. The -p, or protect, flag keeps UNIX from overwriting a file you already have.
sz *filename*	Sends the file from the host computer or program to your computer, using **Zmodem.** Windows automatically receives the file. The MS-DOS filename wildcards ? and * may also be used to receive multiple files.
sz -e *filename*	Sends the file to you, replacing all control characters with **escape characters.**
sz -b *filename*	Sends the file in binary format. Sometimes, if you're having problems sending or receiving a file, using this flag can help solve them.
sz -n *filename*	Sends the file only if there is no file by that name in the receiving directory. Also sends the file if there is a file by that name, but the file being sent is newer, in which case the file being sent replaces the old file.
sz -p *filename*	Sends the file only if there is no file by that name in the receiving directory. This keeps UNIX from overwriting a file you already have.

continues

127

UNIX *(continued)*

About the command flags

The *ls* flags may be combined. For example, my standard command for seeing what's in a directory is *ls -Fa*. That way, I can see all of the files in the directory, including dot files, and I can tell whether they're "special" files or "regular" files. The rz and sz flags can also be combined. For instance, suppose you wanted to receive all files with a DOC extension in binary format, but receive them only if files with the same name did not already exist in the receiving directory. In this case, you would enter *sz -bp *.doc*. You must use the correct case with each flag.

> **SEE ALSO   HyperTerminal; Shell Account**

Uploading Files

How you move a file from your PC to the Internet depends on the way you've connected to the Internet. If you've connected with a **PPP** or **SLIP** connection—which is the way you connect if you're using Internet Explorer—you don't need to move a file from your PC to the Internet because your PC is already part of the Internet. (With a PPP or SLIP connection, however, you can move a file to some other Internet **host** using Windows's **FTP** client.) If you're using an **online service** like The **Microsoft Network,** you use whatever commands the online service's client software provides. If you've connected with a **shell account** and what you want to do is move a file to your **Internet service provider,** you use a communications application like HyperTerminal.

> **SEE ALSO   Downloading Files**

URL SEE Uniform Resource Locator

Usenet Newsgroups SEE Newsgroup

Username

When you **log on** to a **network,** the network wants to know your identity. To identify yourself, give your name or username. Your username is also typically the first part of your Internet e-mail address.

> **SEE ALSO   Authentication; Internet Explorer**

Uuencode

As a general rule, e-mail messages and newsgroup articles must be composed entirely of text. This means that you can't include binary files in an e-mail message or newsgroup **article.** You can't e-mail someone a program file because program files aren't text files, for example. And you can't post a picture to a newsgroup because graphics image files aren't text files.

To deal with this limitation, early Internet users created a program called uuencode. Uuencode converts binary files to text files so they can be included in e-mail messages and posted as newsgroup articles. (This is called uuencoding.) It also converts these text files back into binary files. (Some people call this uudecoding.) With uuencode, therefore, you or your computer goes to an extra bit of work to send or receive binary files. But you can do it.

People still use uuencode. You'll see many uuencoded files in Internet **newsgroups,** for example. But with **Outlook Express** (which is what you'll want to use for **e-mail** and for newsgroup browsing), you don't need to worry about uuencoding or uudecoding binary files. Outlook Express automatically does this for you.

SEE ALSO   MIME

Viewer

To look at a graphics file, such as a **GIF** or **JPEG** file, or to look at a movie file, such as a **MPEG** file or AVI file, you need a viewer. A viewer is just a program that opens graphics files and movie files. Windows comes with a viewer that lets you look at AVI files, the Multimedia Player. **Internet Explorer** comes with an internal viewer that lets you look at GIF and JPEG files. To open an MPEG file, you need an MPEG viewer.

You can often find **shareware** and freeware viewers in the *alt.binaries.utilities* newsgroup and at the *http://www.zdnet.com/* web site.

SEE ALSO   Encoded Files

Virus

A virus is a program created by a pathetic little wimp with a bit of technical knowledge but zero maturity, zero common sense, and zero morals. The virus program this loser creates often attempts to destroy either your computer or the data stored on your computer's hard disk.

You get viruses by using infected floppy disks or infected software on your computer. You also get viruses by **downloading** infected **files** from the Internet.

If your machine does get a virus or if you're wondering whether your machine has one, you can probably locate and eradicate it by using an anti-virus program. You can usually get evaluation copies of anti-virus programs from the *http://www.mcafee.com/* and the *http://www.thunderbyte.com/* web sites.

VT100

Many years ago, Digital Equipment Corporation, a computer hardware manufacturer, created a terminal called the VT100. Because this terminal was so popular, it became a sort of de facto terminal standard. As a result, many terminals (and personal computers that emulate terminals) must pretend to be VT100s when they connect to **BBSs** (bulletin board systems) and Internet service providers. And, more important, the Windows's **telnet** client emulates a VT100 terminal when you use it for Telnet sessions.

I mention this here because if you don't want the telnet client to emulate a VT100 terminal, you need to slightly change the way telnet works. To do this, start the telnet client (if necessary) and then choose the Terminal menu's Preferences command. When telnet displays the Preferences dialog box, use its boxes and buttons to tell telnet which type of terminal it should emulate.

W³ SEE World Wide Web

WAIS

WAIS is an acronym for Wide Area Information Server. But you don't really need to know that. What you should know is that WAIS, pronounced "ways," works sort of like **Gopher.** And in fact you'll sometimes see Gopher menu commands that let you connect to and use WAIS to search through indexes of topics maintained by its **server**.

Wallet

Microsoft Wallet lets you safely store your address and payment information on your computer so that it's easier to shop online. Wallet, then, saves you time because you enter this information only once. Or at least this is true if the online store where you shop knows about Wallet.

Storing Shipping Information with Wallet

To store shipping information with Wallet, follow these steps:

1 Start Internet Explorer if necessary.

2 Choose the View menu's Internet Options command. Internet Explorer displays the Options dialog box.

3 Click the Content tab.

4 Click the Addresses button. Internet Explorer displays the Address Options dialog box.

5 Click the Add button. Internet Explorer displays the Add A New Address dialog box.

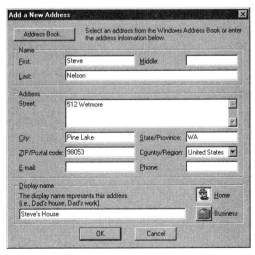

6 Enter the address information in the boxes provided by the Add A New Address dialog box.

continues

131

Wallet *(continued)*

Storing Credit Card Information with Wallet

To store credit card information with Wallet, follow these steps:

1 Start Internet Explorer if necessary.

2 Choose the View menu's Internet Options command. Internet Explorer displays the Options dialog box.

3 Click the Content tab.

4 Click the Payments button. Internet Explorer displays the Payment Options dialog box. (Internet Explorer may prompt you to install the credit card extensions; to do this, simply click the Install button.

5 Click the Add button. Internet Explorer displays the Add menu. Then choose a credit card from the menu.

6 When Internet Explorer asks you to read the licensing agreement, do so. Assuming you agree to the licensing terms, click the I Agree button. Wallet starts the Add A New Credit Card wizard which walks you through the steps of describing a credit card you want to use with Wallet.

WAN

Do network acronyms ever stop? I guess not. WAN stands for wide area network, as in a **network** that includes computers across the state, province, shire, or country.

SEE ALSO   LAN; MAN

Web SEE World Wide Web

Web Browsing

To browse the **World Wide Web**, you first make a **Dial-Up Networking** connection and then you use Internet Explorer to open and display World Wide Web documents.

Starting Internet Explorer

To start Internet Explorer, you just double-click the Internet Explorer icon, which appears on your **desktop.** If necessary, Internet Explorer makes a Dial-Up Networking connection. (You may need to provide information such as your **username** or **password** to make this connection.) After Internet Explorer makes the connection, it downloads and then displays your **start page.**

Note that if you're already connected to the Internet—say because you're already using another Internet **client**—you won't need to make the connection again. So you won't see the dialog box that provides your username, password, and Internet service provider's telephone number.

Viewing the World Wide Web

Once you've loaded your start page, you can view it by scrolling up and down. To move to another World Wide Web document, you click a **hyperlink** in the currently displayed document. (The mouse pointer changes to a pointing finger whenever it rests over a hyperlink.) You can also move to another World Wide Web document by entering a new **uniform resource locator** in the Address box. To move back and forth between World Wide Web pages you've already viewed, click the Back and Forward buttons.

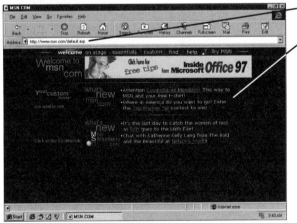

This is the Address box.

This is a World Wide Web document.

Viewing Graphics with Internet Explorer

Internet Explorer comes with **GIF** and **JPEG** viewers built right into it. If you're viewing a World Wide Web document that shows a graphics image, it's usually a GIF file. Sometimes you can click the GIF image or its icon to move to a full-screen JPEG image. (You'll be able to tell when this is the case. The status bar of Internet Explorer will say that the image is a shortcut to some other file.)

continues

Web Browsing *(continued)*

Why the image changes

If you look closely, you'll notice that some graphics images in World Wide Web documents look fuzzy at first but then become more and more focused. What you're seeing, just in case you care, is something called progressive rendering: as the World Wide Web server sends its image to your PC, your PC keeps drawing a better and clearer image the more information it gets.

Printing World Wide Web Documents

Internet Explorer's File menu provides a Print command. You can use it to print the Web document shown in the Internet Explorer window. To use the File Print command, display the Web page you want to print, choose the command, and then click OK when Internet Explorer displays the Print dialog box.

Saving World Wide Web Documents and Images

Internet Explorer's File menu also provides a Save As command. You can use it to save the World Wide Web page you see on your screen. To use this command, just choose it. When Internet Explorer displays the Save HTML Document dialog box, use the File Name box to name the document. (You can also use the Save In box to specify where the web page should be saved.)

You can save full-screen GIF and JPEG images displayed in the Internet Explorer window by choosing the File menu's Save As command. When Internet Explorer displays the Save Picture dialog box, use the Save In and File Name boxes to specify where you want the file saved and what you want it named.

To view a GIF or JPEG file you've previously saved to disk using Internet Explorer, choose the File menu's Open command. When Internet Explorer displays the Open dialog box, click the Browse command button. When Internet Explorer displays the Open dialog box, first activate the Files Of Type box and select either the GIF or JPEG file type, and then use the Look In and File Name box to locate and identify the file.

Disconnecting from the Internet

To disconnect your PC from the Internet, simply stop the Internet client programs you've started. Windows then asks if you want to disconnect from your Internet service provider. Indicate that you do by clicking the Disconnect button.

SEE ALSO   **FTP; Gopher; Internet Explorer; Quick Reference: Internet Explorer Commands *and* Internet Explorer Toolbar Guide; Telnet**

WebCrawler SEE Search Engine

Web Page

Web page is another name for the HTML document you view using a web browser like Internet Explorer. The World Wide Web, as you can guess, is made up of these web pages.

Web Publisher

A web publisher is just someone who creates **web pages** and then places, or publishes, these web pages on a web **server** so that other people can view them. If you're considering becoming a web publisher, by the way, you should know two essential pieces of information. First of all, the actual work of creating web pages and then publishing them isn't difficult. **Internet Explorer** even comes with a simple web creation tool called Microsoft **FrontPage Express** and a handy web publishing tool called **Web Publishing Wizard.** A second thing you should know is that the really hard work of publishing a web page is creating or locating the information you want to share with your web pages.

Web Publishing Wizard

The Web Publishing Wizard lets you publish **HTML** documents, or web pages, to a web **server** that's part of an **intranet** or maintained by your **Internet service provider.** Once you've created your web pages (perhaps using Microsoft **FrontPage Express**), you start the wizard by clicking the Start button and then choosing Programs, Internet Explorer, and then Web Publishing Wizard. To use the wizard, just follow the on-screen instructions.

Web Site

Web site can refer to a couple of things. In this book, I use it to refer to a collection of web pages that a web publisher has created. Microsoft, for example, has a Microsoft Investor web site that provides a bunch of web pages with information of interest to investors. The United States Internal Revenue Service has a web site that provides information of interest to taxpayers.

Some people also use the term *web site* to refer to a web **server.** I don't think, however, that this is a good way to use the term. It makes more sense (to me at least) to just call a web server a web server.

White Pages

White-pages web sites are like electronic address books. You can use white pages to look up someone's **e-mail address** or even their real address and telephone number. One of the largest white pages is Bigfoot, which you can use and learn more about by visiting the web site at *http:/bigfoot/*. Several search engines have their own white and yellow pages. You can also use a search engine to search on the phrase "white pages" for a list of other white pages.

Wildcard Characters

Wildcard characters stand in for other characters in an expression. For example, you can use wildcard characters to stand in for characters in a **filename** when you're searching for a **file,** and you can use them as part of a command. The most common wildcard characters are the question mark (?) and asterisk (*) symbols. A question mark can stand for any single character. An asterisk can stand for any single character, any group of characters, or for no group of characters at all. For example, if you are connected to an **Internet service provider** that runs **UNIX** on its computer and you want to send all of the files in a directory using the send **Zmodem** command *sz,* you could type:

```
sz *
```

Windows Explorer

Windows Explorer lets you do things: It lets you view and work with your computer's disks and the **files** that are stored on your disk. It also lets you view and work with the other parts of your computer—its fonts, Control Panel, and your printer.

Starting Windows Explorer

To start Windows Explorer, click the Start button. Then choose Programs and Windows Explorer. The Windows Explorer window appears.

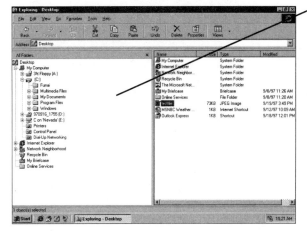

Windows Explorer uses a **folder pane** to show the **folder** structure.

Windows Explorer uses a **file pane** to show the **subfolders** and the files in the active folder. Windows Explorer provides file information, including the file size in **kilobytes** and the last modification date. (The last modification date is the date someone last fiddled with the file by changing its contents.)

Selecting Disks

To select a disk, click on the disk icon in the folder pane.

Selecting Folders

To select a folder, scroll through the folder pane until you see the folder you want. Then click the folder.

If the folder is a subfolder in another folder, you may need to first select the parent folder and display its subfolder. You do this by clicking the parent folder.

Windows Explorer alerts you to subfolders

Windows Explorer adds the plus sign (+) to a folder icon if the folder it represents has subfolders.

continues

Windows Explorer *(continued)*

Selecting Files

To select a file in the active folder, scroll through the file pane until you see the file. Then click it.

You can select more than one file at once by clicking on the first file, holding down the Shift key, and then clicking on the last file. Or you can hold down the Ctrl key and click each file you want to select.

Opening Files

To open a file in the active folder, scroll through the file pane until you see the application or document. Then double-click the file. When you double-click an application, Windows starts the application. When you double-click a document, Windows starts the application in which the document was created and tells the application to open the document you clicked.

WinZip

WinZip is the name of a popular, easy-to-use compression utility. WinZip, like PKZIP, scrunches files so that they take less time to transmit. You can usually find a evaluation copy of WinZip at any web site that provides shareware. For example, you can always find a copy at *http://www.zdnet.com.*

Working Offline SEE Offline

World Wide Web

The World Wide Web (also known as W^3, the Web, and WWW) is a set of multimedia documents that are connected so that you can jump from one document to another by way of hypertext links, usually with a click of a mouse. If this definition sounds complicated, it's probably because I've used a few terms you may not know: document, multimedia, and hypertext. Let me define these terms for you and make the whole picture clear.

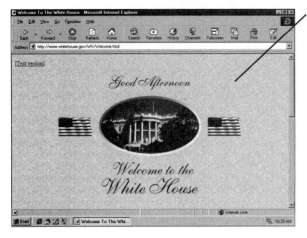

This is the White House's World Wide Web document.

Let's start with the key term, *document*. A document is a report that describes something. Often, documents are on paper. In fact, you've probably created hundreds of paper documents: book reports in grade school; thank-you letters to distant, gift-giving relatives; and perhaps lengthy term papers in college. You wrote these documents on paper, but if you had produced and displayed them on a computer screen, they still would have been documents, right? So now you know what I mean by document.

The *multimedia* part relates to the fact that when you create and display a document on a computer, you aren't limited to words. You can place pictures in a document, for example. And you can place sound objects. Just about any object a computer can create, display, or play can be placed in a document. So now you know what I mean by multimedia.

And now we come to what makes the World Wide Web unique— the *hypertext* part. Hypertext is a connection, oftentimes called a **hyperlink,** that lets you jump from one document to another. Suppose you're reading a document that talks about the U.S. Department of Commerce and what it does. This document references, let's say, the Office of the President with a hypertext connection, or hot link. You click on the words "Office of the President" and see a new document that talks about the president.

continues

World Wide Web *(continued)*

So to return to the original definition, the World Wide Web is simply a set of multimedia documents that are connected using hypertext links. And by clicking on these hyperlinks, you can jump from one document to the next.

Before I finish this discussion, I should make two more points. First of all, to view a World Wide Web document, you need to have a web browser such as **Internet Explorer** (the focus of this book) or **Netscape Navigator.** Second, if you're new to the World Wide Web and don't know where to begin, start with the web site *http:// www.yahoo.com.* It provides a directory of thousands of different World Wide Web servers.

If you want to get technical about hot links, read this

The documents you read, or view, with a web browser are written using something called **HTML.** In fact, the web browser client uses HTML instructions to display a document on your screen. These HTML instructions also include **uniform resource locators.** And when you click a **hot link,** the web browser client uses the uniform resource locator and the Hypertext Transfer Protocol, or **HTTP,** to find and display the other document.

WWW SEE World Wide Web

Yahoo!

The very popular Yahoo! web site essentially amounts to a directory of Internet web sites and pages. In other words, Yahoo! works much like a table of contents in a book. To use Yahoo!, you first look through the Yahoo! directory's main headings to find an information category. Then you click the category's **hyperlink** to see the subcategories within the category. Then you click the appropriate subcategory's hyperlink to see the sub-subcategories within the subcategory. You continue this process until you get to a web page or web site with the information you want.

One thing to recognize about Yahoo! is that while it's a search service, its fundamental organization differs from that of an index-style search service like **AltaVista.** An index-style search service, in effect, maintains an index of web sites and pages which you access by using a **search engine.** A directory-style search service like Yahoo!, in effect, maintains a table of contents of web sites and pages which you typically use by exploring categories and subcategories of hyperlinks. (Yahoo! does provide a search engine, too, so this isn't precisely true, but it's a pretty accurate generalization.)

ZIP

ZIP actually refers to a data-compression technique. When people say a **file** is ZIPed, they usually mean it's been compressed using the **PKZIP** or WinZip utility. To use a ZIPed file, you have to unZIP it. If a file has been ZIPed with PKZIP, for example, you have to unZIP it with PKUNZIP.

Zmodem

When you download or upload a file using a **shell account** and communications application like **HyperTerminal,** you need to choose a communications **protocol.** Zmodem, it turns out, is one of the communications protocols you can choose. If this were some dusty undergraduate telecommunications textbook, I'd probably launch into a detailed technical discussion of the Zmodem protocol at this point. But I'll save you the time. The one and only thing you need to know about Zmodem is that if you are using a shell account to move files around, it's a much faster protocol than your other choices.

SEE ALSO   Downloading Files; Uploading Files

Troubleshooting

Got a problem? Starting on the next page are solutions to the problems that sometimes plague new users of Internet Explorer 4.0. You'll be on your way—and safely out of trouble—in no time.

E-Mail

You Don't Know Someone's E-Mail Address

You want to send so-and-so an **e-mail** message, but you don't have their address? Don't feel embarrassed. I think this is probably the most common Internet problem of all. Really. Fortunately, this problem is easy to solve.

Call them and ask

Sounds silly, doesn't it? But this really is the best solution. So go on and do it. You need to get both their **username** and the **domain name**. Once you know these bits of data, you just send your message to:

```
username@domainname
```

For example, if you wanted to send an e-mail message to me at my **Microsoft Network** address, you would send the message to:

```
stphnlnlsn@msn.com.
```

stphnlnlsn is my Microsoft Network username. And *msn.com* is The Microsoft Network domain name. If you're wondering where in the world I got my username, it's just my first name, middle initial, and last name, without any vowels.

Ask them to e-mail you so you can reply

Another easy gambit is to have the person e-mail you. You need to know your e-mail address so you can tell them. But if they can send you an e-mail message, you'll know their e-mail address and be able to reply. You can, for example, click the Reply To Author button as you're reading their message to display a new message window, already addressed to the person. Or you can right-click their name in the message window so that Microsoft **Outlook Express** displays a shortcut menu. When you see the shortcut menu, choose the Add To Address Book command to tell Outlook Express you want to permanently record the person's e-mail address in your **Address Book.**

E-mail the user's postmaster

If for some reason you can't call the person or contact them some other way—maybe a quick letter—you can also try e-mailing a request to the postmaster at the e-mail post office that serves the **host** on which your friend is a user. I'm not really sure this will work, by the way. Sometimes it will, sometimes it won't. What you're really doing is asking for a special favor from the person who administers the e-mail messaging system for the domain. But to do this, you can usually e-mail your message to:

```
postmaster@domainname
```

Of course, this means you need to know the domain name. So you may need to call the organization for that. But let's say you want to e-mail a message to an old school chum. You know he works for Parnell Aerospace in Taiwan, but you don't know his username. You need to call Parnell Aerospace and get the domain name of the Taiwan office—let's pretend it's *parnell.com.tw*. Then you e-mail your request to the following address:

```
postmaster@parnell.com.tw
```

Conduct a search using a search engine

If you want to contact a person and don't know their address, telephone number, or even if they have an e-mail address, you can use a search engine to find the person's e-mail address if they have one. Several search engines have people search features. All you have to do is display a search engine's home page and see if you can find a hyperlink called people search or something similar. Click on this hyperlink, and then enter all the information you know about the person in the appropriate boxes. If the search turns up empty, try again with a different search engine.

FTP

You Download a File but Can't Access It

If you successfully **download** a file but discover you can't use it, your problem is almost certainly a "mode mixup." What's a mode mixup? When you move files with **FTP**, you move the files either in ASCII mode or in binary mode. Text files need to be moved in ASCII mode. Just about everything else needs to be moved in binary mode. If you use ASCII mode when you should have used binary mode, or vice versa, the file you get won't work right.

Try again, only this time with Microsoft Internet Explorer

If you FTPed a file using the FTP, attempt to download the file again—only this time, use Internet Explorer as the FTP client. In other words, don't use the actual FTP client that comes with Microsoft Windows. To FTP with Internet Explorer, enter the FTP site's uniform resource locator into Internet Explorer's address box, move to the directory that holds the file, and then click the file once you find it. (Note, by the way, that not all FTP servers let you FTP with a web browser. Most do. But some don't.)

Try again with a different transfer mode

If you FTPed a file using the wrong mode, you can't do anything with the downloaded file. It's garbage. You may as well delete the downloaded file. Then try again using a different transfer mode. If you're not sure which transfer mode to use to download a file, take a peek at the table shown on the next page. It lists my suggestions as to the best transfer mode to use for different kinds of files.

File	Type
ARC files	Binary
Database files	Binary
E-mail messages	ASCII
GIF files	Binary
Hypertext documents	ASCII
JPEG files	Binary
MPEG files	Binary
PKZIP files	Binary
PostScript files	ASCII
Program files	Binary
Source code files	ASCII
Spreadsheet files	Binary
Text files	ASCII
Uuencoded files	ASCII
Word processor files	Binary

To set the transfer mode when you're moving a file using FTP, use either the *ascii* command or the *binary* command. Type *ascii* to set the transfer mode to ASCII, of course. And type *binary* to set the transfer mode to binary.

World Wide Web

You Can't Connect to a Web Server

If you can't connect to a web server, either you've got the **uniform resource locator** (URL) wrong or the web server isn't allowing you to connect—perhaps because it's overworked and cranky. Unfortunately, both problems produce the same symptoms.

 ### Check the URL

Carefully check the URL. The first part of the URL should be *http://*. So make sure you've entered this part right. Note that the slashes are really slashes and not backslashes. The server name will probably look something like this: *www.microsoft.com*. In other words, it usually starts with the acronym *www* and then is followed by the web server owner's **domain name.** So to connect to Microsoft Corporation's web server, you enter *http:// www.microsoft.com*. (Of course, if you're connecting to some other company's web server, you don't enter *microsoft*.)

 ### Be patient

Even if you've got the URL entered correctly, you still may not be able to connect. If you get a message when you try to connect to a web server that says something like "host not responding" or "host connection failed," it may just be that the web server isn't available or is too busy to respond.

In this situation, your only real recourse is to try later. If the web server is just really busy, by the way, you might be able to connect a few minutes later.

Your Connection Speed Is Slow

Bandwidth is the practical problem of the Internet and especially of the World Wide Web. The problem is that even with a fast modem, downloading web pages with lots of pretty pictures takes time. Add animation or sound to a web page, and minutes turn into hours—or so it seems. Fortunately, you can do things on your end to minimize the time you spend waiting.

Do something else while you wait

Perhaps the simplest thing to do is just to do something else. Remember that Windows lets you **multitask.** What this means is that you can write that report that's due tomorrow while you're waiting for a web page to download.

 ### Subscribe to a web page

You can subscribe to a web page. When you subscribe to a web page, all it means is that you've told Internet Explorer that you want it to grab updated copies of a web page every so often—such as during the middle of the night while you're sleeping or while you're off at lunch. (Note, therefore, that a **subscription** doesn't cost you anything.) When you later want to view web pages you've subscribed to, you work **offline** and view copies stored on your local disk.

 ### Add an active channel for the web page

Some web sites support **channels.** When a web site does support channels, you can tell the web site that it should routinely send you updated copies of a web page. To do this, click the Add Active Channel button, which you'll see on web pages that can be turned into active channels.

Differentiating between subscriptions and channels

Subscriptions and channels can be a little confusing at first, but they're really quite simple conceptually. Consider the following: The traditional way of moving content from a web server to your PC is by clicking a hyperlink or supplying a uniform resource locator. In other words, you give the instruction to move content from a server to a client. With subscriptions, in comparison, you can tell Internet Explorer to automatically issue an instruction to move content from a server to a client. And with channels, the web site (without instruction from you or Internet Explorer) moves content from a server to a client.

continues

Your Connection Speed Is Slow *(continued)*

 View text-only versions of web pages

The textual portion of a web page doesn't actually take very long to download. Or at least that's usually the case. Therefore, if what you're really interested in is a web page's textual information and a web server gives you the option, you can indicate that you want to view text-versions of a web site's pages. To do this, you typically click a hyperlink that's labeled something like "text-only."

Web Page Pictures Look Gritty

Let's say you're viewing web pages, but your pictures look gritty. You can sort of make out what you're supposed to see, but the pictures are nowhere close to being photograph quality. This, you're wondering to yourself, is what everybody is getting so excited about?

 Increase the number of colors and the resolution

To view photographic images on your monitor, you need to use a SuperVGA monitor. SuperVGA monitors provide greater resolution and display more colors. And you need to tell Windows to use high resolution and lots of color. You probably have a SuperVGA monitor if you purchased your monitor anytime in the last few years. But there's a good chance that you're not using its high resolution and color capabilities. To make sure you are, follow these steps:

1 Right-click the Windows desktop. Windows displays a menu of commands related to the **desktop.**

2 Choose the Properties command. Windows displays the Display Properties dialog box.

3 Click the Settings tab.

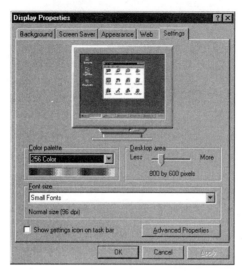

4 If the Color Palette drop-down list box shows 16 Color, select a higher color setting, such as 256 color, High Color (16-bit), or True Color (24-bit). The higher the color setting you choose, the more colors you'll see and the better the image quality will be.

5 Move the Desktop Area slider to the right to increase the resolution.

6 Click OK. Windows may ask if it can reboot your computer so the display setting changes can take effect. Save any unsaved work and then go ahead and do this.

Try another web page

Some of the pictures that are used in web pages aren't high-quality photographic images. So if you've verified that you're using a lot of color and a high resolution, view some other web pages. Quite likely the grittiness you're seeing is in the images themselves and is not the result of a problem with your computer or viewer.

Telnet

You Can't Connect to a Host

If you can't connect to a **host** using the **Telnet** service, your problem probably boils down to one of two things: either you've got the **uniform resource locator** (URL) wrong or the telnet host isn't allowing you to connect. One of these situations you can do something about. The other you can't.

Check the URL

If you get a message when you try to connect to a telnet host that says something like "host unknown," you've got the wrong URL. Plain and simple. So what you need to do is figure out the right URL. Check your source document. Make sure you've entered it exactly as shown. If you did enter it correctly, either your source document is wrong or, just as likely, your source document is out of date.

Be patient

If you get a message when you try to connect to a telnet host that says something like "host not responding" or "host connection failed," it may just be that the telnet host isn't available right now. If you're trying to connect at some really crazy hour (like 3 AM) or when the telnet host is really busy (like during prime business hours), the telnet host is quite likely not available.

In this situation, your only real recourse is to try later. If you know what the telnet host's usual hours of operation are and you know that the telnet host is available, you might want to try again in, say, 10 minutes. If you're trying to connect to a telnet host that you don't know much about or you're trying to connect at some crazy hour, it might be best to wait until normal working hours.

You Connect but Can't Log On or Issue Commands

This happened to me just the other day, in fact. I was showing the Internet to a friend. He wanted to telnet to a library in Minnesota. Proudly I typed in the **uniform resource locator**. A few seconds later, the host we were trying to connect to responded. It asked for our **username** and a **password**. It was weird. I typed these in, successfully logged on, but then couldn't issue any commands. The telnet host told me to type, for example, *HELP* to get a list of commands. So I typed *help*, but nothing happened. It told me I could type *MENU* to get a menu of commands. So I typed *menu*. Again, nothing.

Pay attention to whether your commands and entries should be uppercase or lowercase

You've probably already figured out what I was doing wrong. The case was important. The telnet host wanted the word *HELP* and *MENU* in all uppercase letters. A command name in all lowercase letters like *help* or *menu* just wouldn't do the trick.

Actually, as a general comment, I'll also note that anytime you log on to a **server** running **UNIX,** the case is relevant. If the server wants all lowercase letters—and that's what it usually wants—you better type them. And sometimes, when things are really crazy, the server wants uppercase letters. You had better type them, too.

You Can Issue Commands but You Don't See Them or You See Each Letter Twice

In the previous section, I started to tell you about the embarrassing little episode of telnetting to a library in Minnesota. I have to tell you what happened next. As soon as I figured out the uppercase vs. lowercase business, I could type commands and get the telnet host to do what I wanted it to. But when I typed the command, I wouldn't see it on the command prompt. I would type *HELP*, for example, but I wouldn't see anything. After I pressed the Enter key, however, I would see a screenful of help information. My friend, I feared, was rapidly losing confidence both in the telnet service and in my abilities as a guide to the Internet.

You Can Issue Commands but You Don't See Them or You See Each Letter Twice *(continued)*

 ### Adjust the local echo setting

What was wrong? The local echo setting. In my case, the telnet client, Windows's Telnet program, needed to have the local echo setting turned on. To do this, choose the Terminal Preferences command. Then select the Local Echo check box.

By the way, if you have local echo turned on when it should be turned off, you get double letters for just about everything. Rather than seeing a message like this:

```
Type HELP
```

You see a message like this:

```
TTyyppee HHEELLPP
```

If you get double letters, you should try turning off the local echo setting.

You Can't Disconnect from a Host

Once you've telnetted to a host, you're connected. You need to disconnect from it to get back to the host where you started. Disconnecting isn't difficult. But you do need to know the secret command or escape sequence to disconnect from the host.

 ### Backtrack through the session log

When you initially connected to the host, the host almost certainly told you how to disconnect. Therefore, you may be able to scroll backward and read the stuff you should have read when you first connected. The telnet client, by default, only keeps the last 25 lines or so in its application window. But you may as well try scrolling backward. Click above the Telnet window's scroll bar marker to scroll backward.

 ### Try all the old standbys

To quit whatever you're doing on the host computer, you can probably type an **escape character.** You might try Ctrl+]. You might also try Ctrl+C.

Quick Reference

Any time you explore a new program, you're bound to see features and tools you can't identify. To be sure you can identify the commands and toolbar buttons you see in Internet Explorer 4.0, Outlook Express, and Windows Internet clients, this Quick Reference describes these items in systematic detail.

FTP Client Commands

Command	Description
!	Escapes to the shell.
?	Prints help information about the FTP client application.
append	Appends one file to another (e.g., *append file1 file2* tacks file1 onto the end of file2).
ascii	Sets the file transfer type to ASCII so you can send or receive an ASCII, or text, file.
bell	Tells the FTP client to sound a bell or buzzer whenever it completes a command. (To turn off the bell, issue the bell command again.)
binary	Sets the file transfer type to binary so you can send or receive a binary file.
bye	Terminates an FTP session and closes the FTP client application.
cd	Changes the working directory on the host you FTPed to. (This pretty much works like the MS-DOS command of same name.)
close	Terminates an FTP session without closing the FTP client application.
debug	Turns on or off the FTP's debugging mode.
delete	Deletes a *file* on the host you FTPed to.
dir	Lists the contents of the working directory on the host you FTPed to. (Works like the MS-DOS command of same name.)
disconnect	Terminates an FTP session without closing the FTP client application.
get	Retrieves a specified file from the working directory of the host you've FTPed to (e.g., *get file1* retrieves the file named *file1* from the remote host and then stores it in the working directory of your PC).
glob	Turns metacharacter expansion of local file names on or off.
hash	Turns the printing of a pound sign (#) for each buffer transferred on or off.
help	Displays a list of commands. (If you type *help* followed by the command name, help displays a short command description.)

Command	Description
lcd	Changes the local host's working directory—in other words, the active directory on your PC.
literal	Sends arbitrary FTP commands.
ls	lists the contents of the remote host's working directory. Similar to the DIR command.
mdelete	Deletes a group of (multiple) files on the remote host.
mdir	Lists the contents of multiple directories on the remote host.
mget	Retrieves multiple files from the remote host.
mkdir	Makes a directory on the remote host. (Works like the MS-DOS command of the same name.)
mls	lists the contents of multiple directories on the remote host.
mput	Sends multiple files.
open	Connects to a remote FTP site.
prompt	Tells FTP to interactively prompt you when you're issuing multiple commands.
put	Sends a file.
pwd	Displays the name of the working directory on the remote host.
quit	Terminates the FTP session and closes the FTP client application.
quote	Sends arbitrary FTP commands.
recv	Receives a file.
remotehelp	Gets help from the remote host.
rename	Renames a file. (Works like the MS-DOS command of the same name.)
rmdir	Removes directory on the remote host.
send	Sends a file.
status	Shows the current status of the FTP session.
trace	Turns the tracking of packets on or off.

continues

FTP Client Commands *(continued)*

Command	Description
type	Sets the file transfer type.
user	Sends new information about you to the remote host.
verbose	Turns the verbose mode on or off.

Internet Explorer Commands

File Menu

New	Displays the New submenu.
Window	Opens a new Microsoft Internet Explorer browser window.
Message	Opens a New Message window so you can write an e-mail message.
Post	Opens a New Message window so you can post an article to a newsgroup.
Contact	Opens the Address Book so you can describe a new contact.
Internet Call	Starts Microsoft NetMeeting so you can make an Internet Call.
Open...	Displays a dialog box you use to provide the URL of a web page (or other Internet resource) you want to view using Internet Explorer.
Save	Saves any changes you've made to the open web page.
Save As...	Saves current web page to your hard disk.
Page Setup...	Specifies how web pages should be printed.
Print...	Prints the current web page.
Send	Displays the Send submenu.
Page By E-Mail...	Opens a New Message window (so you can write an e-mail message) and then attaches a copy of the open web page to the message.
Link By E-Mail...	Opens a New Message window (so you can write an e-mail message) and then includes the URL for the open web page in the message.

S̲hortcut To Desktop	Creates a shortcut icon that points to the open web page and then places the shortcut icon on your desktop.
P̲roperties	Displays a Properties dialog box describing the open web page.
W̲ork Offline	A toggle switch, which if marked, tells Internet Explorer to show cached copies of web pages rather than download and then show new copies of web pages.
C̲lose	Closes the Internet Explorer window.

About the other File menu commands

The File menu also lists as commands the web sites you've visited during the current web session. To move to one of these web sites, choose its menu command.

E̲dit Menu

Cu̲t	Removes the current selection and places it on the Clipboard so you can paste the selection somewhere else.
C̲opy	Makes a copy of the current selection and places the copy on the Clipboard so you can paste the selection somewhere else.
P̲aste	Moves the selection currently stored on the Clipboard to the insertion point.
Select A̲ll	Selects all the text in the window.
Page	Allows you to edit the current page using Microsoft FrontPage Express (if you installed the full version of Internet Explorer).
F̲ind...	Searches for specified text on the current web page.

V̲iew Menu

T̲oolbars	Displays the Toolbars submenu.
S̲tandard Buttons	Adds or removes the toolbar of standard buttons. (Internet Explorer also marks the command with a check mark when the buttons are present.)
A̲ddress Bar	Adds or removes the URL address bar from the window. (Internet Explorer marks the command with a check mark when the address bar is present.)

continues

View Menu *(continued)*

Links	Adds or removes Links bar from the window. (Internet Explorer marks the command with a check mark when the Links bar is present.)
Text Labels	Adds or removes text labels from the Internet Explorer toolbars. (Internet Explorer marks the command with a check mark when the Links bar is present.)
Status Bar	Adds or removes a status bar from the window. (Internet Explorer also marks the command with a check mark when the status bar is present.)
Explorer Bar	Displays the Explorer bar submenu.

Search	Opens the Search bar.
Favorites	Opens the Favorites bar.
History	Opens the History bar.
Channels	Opens the Channels bar.
None	Closes the Search, Favorites, History, or Channel bar you've previously opened.

Fonts	Displays the Fonts submenu, which lets you choose a larger or smaller font and change the alphabet for the language of the web site.
Stop	Tells Internet Explorer to stop whatever it's doing—such as retrieving a web page.
Refresh	Tells Internet Explorer to read the web page again (from the web server) and then redraw the window.
Source	Displays the HTML instructions that create the web page.
Full Screen	Uses (almost) the full screen to show the web page by removing Internet Explorer's menu bar and application window title bar. (To return to the regular screen view, click the Full screen button.)
Internet Options...	Displays the Internet Options dialog box so you can specify how Internet Explorer works.

Go Menu

Back	Goes back to the previous web page.
Forward	Goes forward to the next web page.
Up One Level	When you're using Internet Explorer to browse through folders and disks on your local computer or network, displays the contents of the current folder's next higher (or parent) folder.
Home Page	Opens your home, or start, web page.
Channel Guide	Opens Microsoft's Channel Guide web page.
Search The Web	Opens Microsoft's search form web page, which lets you search the Internet using any of the popular search engines.
Mail	Starts your e-mail client (probably Microsoft Outlook Express).
News	Starts your newsgroup reader client (probably Outlook Express).
My Computer	Displays the items—folders, shortcut icons, documents, and so forth—on your desktop in an Internet Explorer window.
Address Book	Starts the Address Book program.
Internet Call	Starts NetMeeting.

Favorites Menu

Add To Favorites...	Adds the current web page location to a list of favorite pages.
Organize... Favorites	Displays the Organize Favorites dialog box, which you can use to reorder, rename, or delete your favorite web pages.
Manage Subscriptions...	Displays a window listing your subscriptions, which you can use to make subscription changes.
Update All Subscriptions	Retrieves updated copies of those web pages you've sub-scribed to.

About the other Favorites menu commands

The Favorites menu also lists the favorite pages you've already added by using the Add To Favorites command. To move to one of these pages, choose its menu command.

continues

Help Menu

Contents And Index	Starts the Help program.
Product Updates	Opens a web page that provides new product information.
Web Tutorial	Opens the web tutorial web page.
Online Support	Opens Microsoft's online support web page.
Microsoft On The **W**eb	Displays a submenu listing Microsoft web sites and pages you can visit.
About Internet Explorer	Displays the About Internet Explorer dialog box and gives the available memory and system resources.

Internet Explorer Toolbar Guide

Back	Goes back to the previous web page.
-	Lists the web pages you can move backward to view.
Forward	Goes forward to the next web page.
-	Lists the web pages you can move forward to view.
Stop	Tells Internet Explorer to stop whatever it's doing—such as retrieving a web page from some distant web server.
Refresh	Tells Internet Explorer to read the web page again (from the web server) and then redraw the window.
Home	Opens your web home base, or home page.
Search	Opens your default search engine web page.
Favorites	Displays the Favorites folder, which lists all your favorite web pages.
History	Displays a history of the web sites and pages you've visited using the Explorer bar.
Channels	Displays Microsoft's Channel Guide web page using the Explorer bar.
Fullscreen	Removes the Internet Explorer application window title and menu bar from your screen so there's more space to show the web page.

Displays a menu of commands for reading e-mail, creating new messages, sending web pages or URLs to people via e-mail, and reading newsgroup articles.

Prints the current web page.

Starts FrontPage Express (if you installed the full version of Internet Explorer) so you can edit or view the HTML instructions of the open web page.

Outlook Express Commands

File

Open — Displays contents of the selected folder or e-mail message.

Save As... — Lets you save the selected message.

Save Attachments — Displays a submenu listing the selected message's attachments. To save an attachment, choose its submenu command.

Save As Stationery... — Uses the selected message to create new message stationery.

Folder — Displays the Folder submenu.

New Folder... Creates a new folder.

Rename... Renames the selected folder.

Compact Compresses the selected folder so it does not waste space.

Compact All Folders Compresses all your folders so that they save space.

Move To... Moves a folder to a new location.

Delete Deletes the selected folder.

Import — Displays the Import submenu.

Address Book... Imports names and addresses from another e-mail client's address book.

Messages... Imports messages from another e-mail client.

Mail Account Settings... Imports the mail account settings information used by another e-mail client.

continues

File *(continued)*

Export	Displays the Export submenu.
	Address Book... Exports names and addresses from Outlook Express to another e-mail client's address book.
	Messages... Exports messages from Outlook Express to another e-mail client.
Print...	Prints selected e-mail message.
Connect	Displays a submenu that lists Internet Dial-Up Networking connections you can make to send and receive e-mail.
Hang Up	Terminates the current Dial-Up Networking connection.
Work Offline	A toggle switch, which if marked, tells Outlook Express to show cached copies of messages and newsgroup articles rather than download and then show new copies of web page.
P**r**operties	Displays or changes properties of selected folder or e-mail message.
L**o**g Off	Logs off the current Outlook Express user so another user can log on.
E**x**it	Closes Outlook Express.

The newsgroup version of the File menu

The preceding table lists the commands that appear on the e-mail version of the File menu. If you're working with a newsgroup, Outlook adds the Clean Up Files command for removing articles you have downloaded.

Edit

Copy	Copies the current selection.
Select **A**ll	Selects all the folders or e-mail messages shown in the message pane.
Delete	Deletes the current selection.
Move To Folder...	Moves the selected message to another folder.
Copy To Folder...	Copies the selected message to another folder.
Mar**k** As Read	Marks the selected message as one you've read.

Mark All As R<u>e</u>ad	Marks all the messages in the selected folder as read.
Mark As <u>U</u>nread	Unmarks a message you've previously marked as read.
Find Pe<u>o</u>ple...	Finds a name in your Address Book.
Find <u>T</u>ext....	Finds text in the selected item.
<u>F</u>ind Message...	Finds a message in the selected folder.

The newsgroup version of the Edit menu

The preceding table lists the commands that appear on the e-mail version of the Edit menu. If you're working with a newsgroup, Outlook adds two new commands. It adds the Mark Thread As Read command so that you can mark all the articles that you've read in the selected thread and it adds the Unscramble (ROT13) command so that you can decipher articles that have been scrambled using ROT13 encryption. It also adds the Find Next command so that you can find the next name, text string, or article that matches your search criteria.

View

Current <u>V</u>iew	Displays the Current View submenu.
	<u>A</u>ll Messages Displays all the messages in a folder or newsgroup.
	<u>U</u>nread Messages Displays only the unread messages in a folder or newsgroup.
<u>N</u>ext	Displays the Next submenu.
	<u>N</u>ext Message Displays the next message.
	<u>P</u>revious Message Displays the previous message.
	Next Unread <u>M</u>essage Displays the next unread message.
	Next Unread <u>T</u>hread Displays the next unread thread.
	Next Unread Fol<u>d</u>er Displays the next unread folder.
<u>C</u>olumns...	Displays a dialog box you use to specify what information you want displayed in the message pane.
Sort <u>B</u>y	Displays a submenu with commands and settings that correspond to sort orders and options.

continues

View *(continued)*

Fonts	Displays the Font submenu:	
	Largest	Uses a font that's the next size larger than the "larger" font.
	Larger	Uses a font the next size larger than the "medium" font.
	Medium	Uses the default font size for text in the window.
	Smaller	Uses a font the next size smaller than the "medium" font.
	Smallest	Uses a font that's the next size smaller than the "smaller" font.
Language	Displays a submenu with commands that correspond to the different languages you can use to view messages.	
Toolbar	Turns off and on the display of the toolbar. (Command is checked if toolbar is displayed.)	
Collapse	Hides the replies to the selected message or article.	
Status Bar	Turns off and on the display of the status bar. (Command is checked if status bar is displayed.)	
Layout...	Displays a dialog box you can use to change the appearance of the Outlook Express window.	
Refresh	Tells Outlook Express to read again the messages in a folder or the articles in a newsgroup.	
Stop	Tells Outlook Express to stop whatever it's doing—such as retrieving a message.	

The newsgroup version of the View menu

The preceding table lists the commands that appear on the e-mail version of the View menu. If you're working with a newsgroup, Outlook adds some special commands specifically for working with newsgroups. It adds the Downloaded Messages, Replies To My Posts, and Filtered Messages commands for displaying only certain messages. It also adds the Expand and Collapse commands to display or hide replies to the selected article.

Go Menu

Up One Level	Displays the contents of the current folder's next higher (or parent) folder.
Go To Folder...	Moves to another folder.
Home Page	Opens your home, or start, web page.
Search The Web	Opens Microsoft's search form web page, which lets you search the Internet using any of the popular search engines.
Best Of The Web	Opens Microsoft's list of the best sites on the World Wide Web.
Inbox	Opens your Inbox folder to show its messages.
News	Starts your newsgroup reader client (probably Outlook Express).
Internet Call	Starts NetMeeting.

Tools

Send	Sends all the current messages either to your Internet service provider's mail server if you're connected to the Internet or to your Outbox folder if you're not.
Send And Receive	Displays a submenu that lists Dial-Up Networking connections you can use to pass e-mail messages to and from the Internet. To send and receive messages, you choose a connection.
Download All	Downloads all the messages in a folder
Address Book...	Displays the Address Book, a list of e-mail addresses.
Inbox Assistant...	Lets you describe how the Inbox Assistant should work.
Accounts...	Lets you specify, change, or view the mail, directory, and newsgroup accounts you use with Outlook Express.
Stationery...	Lets you specify which stationery Outlook Express should use for your e-mail messages and the newsgroup articles you post.
Options...	Changes Outlook Express's appearance and operation.

The newsgroup version of the Tools menu

The preceding table lists the commands that appear on the e-mail version of the Tools menu. If you're working with a newsgroup, Outlook changes some of the command names and adds some special commands specifically for downloading articles, downloading newsgroup lists, and filtering newsgroup articles.

Compose

New Message	Opens the New Message window so you can create an e-mail message.
New Message Using	Displays a submenu that lists the stationery you can use for e-mail messages. To create a message with a particular stationery, choose the submenu option that corresponds to the stationery.
Reply To Author	Creates a new message that replies to the sender of the currently displayed message.
Reply To All	Creates a new message that replies to all the recipients of the currently displayed message.
Forward	Sends a copy of the currently displayed message to someone new.
Forward As Attachment	Sends a copy of the currently displayed message as an attachment to someone new.

Help Menu

Contents And Index	Starts the Help program.
Read Me	Displays a small text file with late-breaking information about the Outlook Express program.
Microsoft On The Web	Displays a submenu listing Microsoft web sites and pages you can visit.
Learn About Microsoft Outlook	Displays a Microsoft web page that provides information about Microsoft Outlook, the program upon which Outlook Express is based.
About Microsoft Outlook Express	Displays the About Microsoft Outlook Express dialog box and gives the available memory and system resources.

Outlook Express Toolbar Guide

 Opens the New Message window so you can create an e-mail message.

 Displays a submenu that lists the stationery you can use for e-mail messages.

 Creates a new message that replies to the sender of the currently displayed message.

 Creates a new message that replies to all the recipients of the currently displayed message.

 Sends a copy of the currently displayed message to someone new.

 Connects Outlook Express to your mail server so Outlook Express can send messages you've created and receive messages other people have sent you.

 Deletes the selected item.

 Displays your Address Book.

Telnet Commands

Connect Menu

Remote System... Displays a dialog box for naming the telnet host you want to connect to.

Disconnect Disconnects your PC from the telnet host you're connected to.

Exit Closes, or stops, the Telnet application.

About the numbered Connect menu commands

The Connect menu also lists the last four access providers you connected to using your PPP or SLIP connection. You can tell Telnet you want to connect to one of these remote systems simply by choosing it from the Connect menu.

Edit Menu

Copy	Copies the selected text in the Telnet application window to the Windows Clipboard.
Paste	Pastes the contents of the Windows Clipboard into the Telnet application window.
Select **A**ll	Selects the entire contents of the Telnet application window.

Terminal Menu

Preferences...	Displays a dialog box you can use to specify how the Telnet application window should look and how the Telnet application itself should work.
Start **L**ogging...	Saves all the stuff that appears in the Telnet application window to a log named telnet.log. You can open the log file using a word processor, Notepad, or WordPad.
Stop Logging	Tells Telnet to stop keeping a session log.

Help Menu

Contents	Lists the major help topic categories.
Search For Help On...	Provides help on a topic you specify.
How To Use Help	Provides help on the Help application.
About Telnet...	Displays the copyright notice, the software version number, and system information from your computer.

Special Characters

* (wildcard) 136
? (wildcard) 136

A

access providers. *See* Internet service
    providers
accounts, Internet 16
    See also passwords; usernames;
      shell accounts
active channels. *See also* subscriptions,
    web page
    adding to desktop 36–37
    overview 16–17
    viewing 37
    web pages as 16–17, 149
Active Desktop
    adding web pages to 17–18
    customizing 19
    defined 17
    removing items 19
    switching between Windows desktop
      and browser window 19
    updating items 19
ActiveX 21
Add Active Channel button 36, 37
Address Book 21–25, 144
addresses, e-mail
    adding to Address Book 22–23, 144
    defined 6, 52
    deleting 24
    importing 24
    obtaining 144–45
    printing 23
    searching web for 145
    storing 22–23, 144
    updating 24
    using 23–24
Add To Active Desktop button 17
Advanced Research Project Agency 30
AltaVista 25, 141
    See also search engines
America Online 5, 26

anchors 26
    See also hyperlinks
anonymous FTP 26–27
    See also FTP (file transfer protocol)
Apple Macintosh 27
ARC files 59, 147
Archie
    defined 28
    finding servers 28–29
    using with e-mail 28
    using with Internet Explorer 30
    using with Telnet 28
ARPA
    and CERT 36
    and Internet history 30
articles 30
    See also newsgroups
ASF files 90
attachments
    and e-mail messages 51
    posting to newsgroups 96
    saving from newsgroups 94–95
    split 94–95
authentication 31
    See also passwords; usernames
AVI files, viewing 129

B

backbones 31
bandwidth 31, 148–49
baud 32
BBS 32
binary digits 32
binary mode 147
bitmaps
    defined 33
    GIF files 59, 67, 133
    JPEG files 80, 81, 133
    viewing images 133–34
BITNET 33
bits 32
bits per second (bps) 31, 34
bookmarks 34
    See also Favorites folder
bridges 34

browsers. *See also* Internet Explorer
  and Active Desktop 19
  frames 62
  Netscape Navigator 34, 90
  overview 35
  role of 140
browsing 132–34
bulletin board systems 32
bytes 85

C

cable modems 35
cache. *See* document cache
capital letters. *See* case
case
  in Telnet commands 153
  in URLs 125
CERT (Computer Emergency Response
  Team) 36
Channel bar 16
channels
  active 16–17, 149
  adding to desktop 36–37
  defined 36
  vs. subscriptions 149
CHAP (Challenge Handshake Authenti-
  cation Protocol) 31
Chat 38
circuit-switching networks 38
  See also packet-switching networks
clients 39
codes. *See* encryption
color displays, changing
  properties 150–51
command flags 128
commands
  FTP client 156–58
  Internet Explorer 158–62
  Outlook Express 163–68
commands*(continued)*
  Telnet 169–70
  UNIX 126–27
communications protocols 141
Compose menu (Outlook Express) 168

compression utilities
  defined 10
  PKZIP 104
  WinZip 138
  and ZIP files 105, 141
CompuServe 5, 98
computer viruses 130
connections
  Dial-Up Networking 40, 41–42
  disconnecting from FTP 66
  disconnecting from Internet 134
  disconnecting from Telnet 54,
    124, 154
  host-to-host 3
  HyperTerminal 75
  Internet 4–5
  Internet service providers 4, 5, 78
  overview 39
  PPP (Point-to-Point
    Protocol) 106, 114
  remote 12–13
  shell accounts 111
  SLIP (Serial Line Internet
    Protocol) 113–14
  Telnet 12–13, 122–24
  T1 transmission lines 120–21
  T3 transmission lines 121
Connection Wizard 40
Connect menu (Telnet) 169
cookies 40
crackers 104
credit cards. *See* Microsoft Wallet
cryptography. *See* encryption
cyberspace 40

D

DARPA. *See* ARPA
database files, transfer mode 147
data compression
  amount of compression 105
  PKZIP 104
  WinZip 138
  and ZIP files 105, 141
data transfer modes 146–47

data transmission. *See also* modems
baud 32
bits per second 34
cable modems 35
Ethernet standard 54–55
modem speed 32, 34, 68
T1 transmission lines 120–21
T3 transmission lines 121
Deleted Items folder 50
desktop
and active channels 16, 17
Active Desktop 17–21
adding active channels 36–37
adding web pages to 17–18
defined 17, 41
viewing active channels 37
desktop items 41
Dial-Up Networking
making connections 42
overview 41
setting up connections 40, 42
Dial-Up Scripting Tool 108
digital IDs 42
document cache
adjusting 44
defined 43
flushing 43
documents, web 139–40
See also HTML documents
domain names
and countries 45
host names 73
list of organization types 45
overview 44
Domain Name Service (DNS) 45
See also IP addresses
domains, defined 2
downloading files
overview 46
troubleshooting FTP 146–47
using HyperTerminal 75
using Internet Explorer 46

E

echo setting 154
Edit menu (Internet Explorer) 159
Edit menu (Outlook Express) 164–65
Edit menu (Telnet) 170
electronic mail. *See* e-mail
electronic mailing lists. *See* mailing lists
e-mail. *See also* addresses, e-mail; mailing lists; messages, e-mail
addresses, defined 52
configuring Outlook
Express 46–47
message transfer mode 147
overview 6–7, 46
replying to 50
security of messages 7
sending messages 47, 48
spam 115
troubleshooting 144–45
using Archie with 28
emoticons. *See* smileys
encoded files 52–53
encryption
overview 53
PGP 100–102
ROT13 107–8
escape character 54, 154
Ethernet 54–55
Exchange. *See* Microsoft Exchange
EXE files 59
Explorer bar 55–56

F

FAQ 56
Favorites folder 57–58
See also bookmarks
Favorites menu (Internet
Explorer) 57–58, 161
file extensions 58–59
File menu (Internet Explorer) 158–59
File menu (Outlook Express) 163–64
filenames 59–60
file pane 60, 137

files
defined 58
downloading 46, 146–47
encoded 52–53
finding 11
naming 60
opening using Windows
    Explorer 138
transfer modes 146–47
transferring 10–11
uploading 128
viewing 129
file transfers 10–11
    See also FTP (file transfer protocol)
file types
filename extensions 58–59
transfer modes 146–47
viewing 129, 133
file viewers 129
finding. See also search engines
Archie servers 28–29
files 11
FTP sites 28–30
Gopher resources 69–71
mailing lists 83
finger command 60–61
flags, UNIX 128
flames 61
folder pane 62, 137
folders
defined 61
Deleted Items folder 50
Favorites folder 57–58
subfolders 117
formatting e-mail messages 48
frames 62
freenets 62
free speech 62–63
freeware 110
Frequently Asked Questions 56
FrontPage Express 64, 135
FTP (file transfer protocol)
anonymous 26–27
client software 65, 66
connecting to sites 66
defined 64

FTP (continued)
disconnecting from sites 66
finding sites 28–30
list of client commands 156–58
retrieving files 66
starting session 65
troubleshooting downloads ... 146–47
using Internet Explorer 64, 146
Fullscreen button 9
full screen mode 67

G

gateways 67
GIF files
defined 59, 67
transfer mode 147
viewers 129
viewing images 133–34
vs. JPEG files 80
gigabytes 68
global networks 2
Go menu (Internet Explorer) 161
Go menu (Outlook Express) 167
Gopher
connecting to servers 69
finding resources 69–71
overview 68–69
using 69
graphics images. See also GIF files; JPEG
    files
bitmaps 33
defined 8
saving in Internet Explorer 134
troubleshooting
    appearance 150–51
viewing in Internet
    Explorer 133–34
Gulf War 72

H

hardware. See modems
Help menu (Internet Explorer) 162
Help menu (Outlook Express) 168

Help menu (Telnet) 170
home pages 72
host computers 73
host names 73
hosts 2, 3, 12
hot links 73
     See also hyperlinks
HTML documents. *See also* web pages
   creating using FrontPage
     Express 64, 135
   publishing using Web Publishing
     Wizard 135
   transfer mode 147
   as wallpaper 19–21
HTML (hypertext markup
     language) 73, 140
HTTP (Hypertext Transfer
     Protocol) 74
hyperlinks 8, 74–75, 139
HyperTerminal 75
hypertext. *See* hyperlinks
hypertext documents. *See* HTML
     documents
hypertext markup language
     (HTML) 73, 140
Hypertext Transfer Protocol
     (HTTP) 74

I

images. *See* graphics images
Inbox Assistant 75
installing Internet Explorer 76
Integrated Services Digital Network
     (ISDN) 80
interest lists, defined 6
     See also mailing lists
Internet. *See also* World Wide Web
   connecting to 4–5
   disconnecting from 134
   free speech issues 62–63
   Gopher 68–71
   overview 2–3
   role of ARPA 30
Internet addresses 77
Internet Calls 90

Internet Explorer
   active channels 16
   defined 77
   document cache 43–44
   Explorer bar 55–56
   exploring My Computer
     window 88–89
   file viewer 129
   FrontPage Express add-in 64, 135
   full screen 67
   installing 76
   list of menu commands 158–62
   list of toolbar buttons 162–63
   Microsoft Chat add-in 38
   plug-ins 105
   starting 133
   using Archie with 30
   using for FTP 64, 146
   web browsing 132–34
Internet Protocol (IP) 79
Internet service providers
   accounts 16
   overview 4, 5, 78
Internet Society 79
InterNIC 79
intranets 79
IP addresses 79, 103
IP (Internet Protocol) 79
ISDN (Integrated Services Digital
     Network) 80
ISPs. *See* Internet service providers

J

Java 80
JPEG files
   compressing images 81
   defined 80
   transfer mode 147
   viewers 129
   viewing images 81, 133–34
   vs. GIF files 67
Jughead 71
junk e-mail 115

K

kilobits 81
kilobits per second (Kbps) 31
kilobytes 81, 85

L

LANs 54–55, 82
Library of Congress 54
LISTSERV 82, 84, 85
   See also mailing lists
local echo setting 154
logging on
   defined 82
   passwords 100
   usernames 128
lowercase. *See* case
lurking 82
Lynx program 35

M

Macintosh 27
mail. *See* e-mail; mailing lists; snail mail
mailing lists
   configuring Outlook Express 83
   defined 6, 83
   finding 83
   moderated 87–88
   subscribing to 83, 84
   unsubscribing from 84, 85
Majordomo 84, 85
MAN 85
megabits per second (Mbps) 31
megabytes 68, 85
menu commands
   Internet Explorer 158–62
   Outlook Express 163–68
   Telnet 169–70
menu systems, defined 12
messages, e-mail
   attaching files to 50–51
   creating 47
   deleting 50

messages, e-mail *(continued)*
   formatting 48
   forwarding 49
   holding in Outbox 48
   reading 48–49
   replying to 50
   retrieving 48
   sending from Outbox 48
   transfer mode 147
   using addresses in 23–24
   using stationery 116–17
Microsoft Chat 38
Microsoft Exchange 55
Microsoft FrontPage 64, 135
Microsoft NetMeeting 90
The Microsoft Network 5, 86
Microsoft Wallet 131
MIME protocol 51, 86–87
modems. *See also* Dial-Up Networking
   cable modems 35
   data transmission speed 32, 34, 68
   and HyperTerminal 75
   overview 87
moderators 87–88
monitors 150
MPEG files
   defined 59, 88
   transfer mode 147
   viewing 129
MPG files. *See* MPEG files
MS-DOS 59
multimedia 139
Multimedia Player 129
multitasking 88
My Computer 88

N

names, searching for 145
name servers. *See* Domain Name
   Service (DNS)
naming files 60
Navigator 34, 90
netiquette 89–90
NetMeeting 90
Netscape Navigator 34, 90

NetShow Player 90
Network News Transfer Protocol
   (NNTP) 97
networks
   bridges 34
   circuit-switching 38
   Ethernet standard 54–55
   freenets 62
   LANs 82
   overview 2, 91
   role of Internet 2–3
newbies 91
newsgroups
   articles 30
   configuring Outlook Express as
     reader 92
   FAQs 56
   and free speech 62–63
   moderated 87–88
   overview 7, 91–92
   posting to 93, 95–96
   private replies to postings 95
   reading articles 93–94
   saving attachments 94
   sexually oriented material 96, 110
   subscribing to 92–93
   TIN reader 124
   unsubscribing from 93
NNTP (Network News Transfer
   Protocol) 97
NSFnet 31, 97

O

offline, working 97
online services. *See also* Microsoft Wallet
   America Online 26
   The Microsoft Network 86
   overview 98
   relationship to Internet 5
opening files 138
Outbox 48
outernet 98
Outlook Express. *See also* e-mail
   Address Book 21–25, 144
   configuring as newsgroup reader .. 92

Outlook Express *(continued)*
   configuring for e-mail 46–47
   configuring for mailing lists 83
   defined 6, 98
   Inbox Assistant 75
   list of menu commands 163–68
   stationery 116–17
   toolbars 169

P

packets 99
packet-switching networks 72, 99
PAP (Password Authentication
   Protocol) 31
passwords
   and authentication 31
   and Internet accounts 16
   and logging on 82
   overview 100
people, searching for 145
PGP 100–102
Pine 102
pinging 102–3
pirates 104
PKZIP files 104, 147
plug-ins 105, 106
ports 105
posting articles to newsgroups 93,
   95–96
postmaster 145
PostScript files, transfer mode 147
PPP (Point-to-Point Protocol)
   and authentication 31
   making Dial-Up Networking con-
     nections 42
   overview 106
   setting up Dial-Up Networking
     connections 42
   vs. SLIP 114
Pretty Good Privacy. *See* PGP
printing web documents 134
program files, transfer mode 147
progressive rendering 134

protocols
CHAP (Challenge Handshake Authentication Protocol) 31
defined 106
FTP (file transfer protocol) 64–66
HTTP (Hypertext Transfer Protocol) 74
IP (Internet Protocol) 79
MIME protocol 86–87
PAP (Password Authentication Protocol) 31
PPP (Point-to-Point Protocol) 106, 114
SLIP (Serial Line Internet Protocol) 113
TCP/IP protocol 72
Zmodem communications protocol 141
providers. *See* Internet service providers
publishers, web 135

R

RAS. *See* Remote Access Service
reading e-mail 48–49
RealPlayer 106
Remote Access Service 107
remote connections 12–13
replying to e-mail 50
resolution, image 150
resources 107
    See also URLs
ROT13 107–8
RTFM 108

S

saving web documents 134
scripting 108
search engines
AltaVista 25, 141
defined 108
finding people by searching 145
index-style *vs.* directory-style 141

search engines *(continued)*
list of 109
using 109
Yahoo! 140–41
security issues. *See also* encryption
e-mail 6
pirates 104
role of CERT 36
viruses 130
servers
Archie servers 28–29
defined 110
vs. web sites 135
session log 154
sexually oriented material 96, 110
shareware 110
shell accounts
defined 111
and HyperTerminal 75
and Pine 102
TIN newsgroup reader 124
and Zmodem 141
shopping online. *See* Microsoft Wallet
shortcut icons 111–12
shouting 112
signatures 112–13
    See also digital IDs
SLIP (Serial Line Internet Protocol)
making Dial-Up Networking connections 42
overview 113
setting up Dial-Up Networking connections 42
vs. PPP 114
vs. shell accounts 113
smileys 114
snail mail 115
source code files, transfer mode 147
spam 115
spreadsheet files, transfer mode 147
SprintNet 31
starting Internet Explorer 133
start pages 116
stationery 116
subfolders 117

subscribing
  to mailing lists 83, 84
  to newsgroups 92–93
  to web pages 117–19, 149
subscriptions, web page
  managing list 118
  overview 117
  scheduling updates 118–19
  setting up 117–18
  vs. channels 149
SuperVGA monitors 150
switching tasks 120

T

Taskbar 120
tasks, switching 120
TCP/IP protocol 72, 122
Telnet
  connecting to sites 122–23
  disconnecting from sites 54, 124,
   154
  ending session 124
  importance of case 153
  Library of Congress site 54
  list of menu commands 169–70
  local echo setting 154
  overview 12–13, 122
  session log 154
  starting session 122–23
  troubleshooting 152–54
  using Archie with 28
  using with Internet Explorer 122–23
  using with Telnet client 123
temporary files. *See* document cache
Terminal menu (Telnet) 170
text files
  filename extension 59
  transfer mode 147
threads 124
TIN 124
toolbars
  Internet Explorer 9, 162–63
  Outlook Express 169

Tools menu (Outlook Express) 167
transfer modes, file 146–47
troubleshooting
  e-mail addresses 144–45
  FTP downloads 146–47
  graphic image appearance 150–51
  Telnet 152–54
  URLs 148
  World Wide Web connec-
   tions 148–50
T1 transmission lines 120–21
T3 transmission lines 121
TXT files 59

U

uniform resource locators. *See* URLs
UNIX
  defined 126
  list of commands 126–27
  using wildcards 136
uploading files 128
uppercase. *See* case
URLs
  bookmarks 34
  case in 125
  defined 8, 124
  domain names 44–45
  elements of 125
  Favorites folder 57–58
  list of services and protocols 125
  and ports 105
  troubleshooting 148
Usenet. *See* newsgroups
usernames 16, 128
users, defined 2
UUE files 59
uuencoded files
  and e-mail 51
  file extensions 59
  overview 129
  transfer mode 147

V

Veronica 70–71
viewers 129
View menu (Internet Explorer) 159–60
View menu (Outlook Express) 165–66
viruses 130
VT100 130

W

WAIS 130–31
Wallet 131
wallpaper, HTML documents as 19–21
WANs 132
Web. *See* World Wide Web
web browsing 132–34
   See also browsers
web pages. *See also* channels
   and Active Desktop 17–21
   creating using FrontPage
     Express 64, 135
   defined 135
   on desktop 17–21
   home pages 72
   publishing using Web Publishing
     Wizard 135
   start pages 116
   subscribing to 117–19, 149
   viewing text-only versions 150
web publishers 135
Web Publishing Wizard 135
web sites. *See also* web pages
   as channels 16–17, 36, 149
   search engines 108–9
   vs. web servers 135
white pages 136
wildcard characters 136
Windows desktop. *See* desktop

Windows Explorer
   defined 136
   elements of 137
   file pane 60, 137
   folder pane 62, 137
   making selections 137–38
   opening files 138
   starting 136
WinZip 138
wizards
   Connection Wizard 40
   Web Publishing Wizard 135
word processor files, transfer mode ... 147
working offline 97
World Wide Web. *See also* Internet
   Explorer
   browsing 132–34
   elements of 139
   overview 8–9, 138
   printing documents 134
   saving documents 134
   saving images 134
   troubleshooting connec-
     tions 148–50
   viewing documents 133
WWW. *See* World Wide Web

Y

Yahoo! 140–41

Z

Zimmerman, Phillip 100–102
ZIP files 59, 104–5, 141
Zmodem 141

The manuscript for this book was prepared and submitted to Microsoft Press in electronic form. Text files were prepared using Microsoft Word 97. Pages were composed by Stephen L. Nelson, Inc., using PageMaker 6.01 for Windows, with text in Minion and display type in Univers. Composed pages were delivered to the printer as electronic prepress files.

Cover Designer
Gregory Hickman

Interior Text Designer
Kim Eggleston

Page Layout
Stefan Knorr

Editor
Paula Thurman

Writer
Stephen Nelson

Technical Editor
Kaarin Dolliver

Indexer
Julie Kawabata

Printed on recycled paper stock.